# VILNIUS

VIL

# Tomas Venclova

# NIUS

## City Guide

R. Paknio leidykla

# History of Vilnius

# VILNA LITVANIAE *Metropolis.*

"Wilno was an oddity, a city of mixed-up, overlapping regions, like Trieste or Czerniowce", wrote the Polish poet Czesław Miłosz about Vilnius, where he spent his youth between the two world wars. Even today the city remains an oddity, though its fate has fundamentally changed: now it is no longer a provincial centre ruled by Poland, but the capital of independent Lithuania. After a break of long centuries Vilnius (also called Wilno and Vilna) has now regained its original status and glory: in the 14th century Duke Gediminas founded it as the seat of the Lithuanian State. Later it was one of the two capitals of the Lithuanian-Polish Commonwealth (the other one was Krakow, later Warsaw), the centre of the so-called North Western region occupied by the Russian Empire, and in the 20th century it was transferred from one rule to another many times. Because of historical disasters not only its buildings and streets, but also entire population groups would disappear. The most tragic of all these events was the destruction of a large Jewish community during the Second World War. However, regardless of all the changes of state dependence, cultures and languages, Vilnius has always remained many-faceted and multilingual. It has been and will always be a dialogue city.

Despite wars, occupations and destruction, the architectural ensemble of Vilnius remains unique. A city lacking German or Scandinavian features, rather reminiscent of Prague or Rome, Vilnius differs greatly from the other Baltic capitals. It is the largest Baroque city north of the Alps, and the one farthest to the east. Yet, nearly all styles of European architecture from Gothic to Classicism are present in Vilnius. They used to reach Lithuania belatedly, but probably due to this reason their examples are particularly mature and flawless. Baroque domes and towers of Vilnius coexist with an irregular mediaeval city plan. The spirit of Rome in Vilnius merges with a mix of other cultural influences: the city has always contained a multitude of Russian Orthodox churches, synagogues and even mosques that sometimes imitated Baroque, but more often clung to their own models.

The Lithuanian capital reminds one of a palimpsest – an ancient manuscript in which the text reveals traces of an earlier text or even several of them underneath it. The city is surrounded by a hilly northern landscape: because of abun-

The Great courtyard of the Vilnius University and the Church of St. John.
From *Album de Wilna* by Jan Kazimierz Wilczyński

dant forests and lakes it has always appeared somewhat untamed. Throughout the city, up to its very centre, islands of untamed nature can be found.

Since the Middle Ages Vilnius has been posed on the boundary between Catholicism and Russian Orthodoxy. These two forms of Christianity meet here today, and in a certain sense even interpenetrate each other due to the presence of Uniates (Russian Orthodox believers who acknowledge the supremacy of the Pope). The capital's Catholic tradition manifests itself in the cult of the Holy Virgin Mary of Aušros Gate (Ostra Brama) that has become the basic part of the myth of Vilnius. However, the Reformation has also left its mark in the city, and during the 17th–18th centuries it was probably the most significant centre of Judaism in the world. Small but visible Muslim and Karaite communities existed (and still exist) here. In Europe such a variety of religions can be encountered perhaps only in the Balkans. Yet people of different religious convictions usually coexisted and today coexist quite peacefully in Vilnius. It should be added that Lithuania was the last country in Europe to accept Christianity. Originally Vilnius was a pagan city with a small Christian presence, and in its environs certain pre-Christian traditions persisted almost until our times. Religious differences were accompanied by linguistic ones. Many Vilniusites know several local languages – Lithuanian, Polish, Russian, and quite recently they could express themselves in Belorussian and Yiddish as well.

The two other capitals of the Baltic states – Riga and Tallinn – were, at least initially, colonial cities, founded and ruled by Western conquerors, while Vilnius was built by local residents and drew naturally on its own soil. Besides, it did not belong to the Hanseatic trade association: though it did not lack merchants and craftsmen, Vilnius was first of all a city of rulers, a centre of spiritual life and science. In the Jewish tradition Vilnius is called "the Jerusalem of Lithuania". It has become a kind of Jerusalem, the core of cultural achievements and historical aspirations, for Lithuanians and other local nations as well.

A particular paradox of Vilnius is the circumstance that it is both a capital and a borderline city. It was situated in the western part of the Grand Duchy of Lithuania, close to the border with the Teutonic order, and later in the east of the Lithuanian-Polish Commonwealth, being something like a node of the Catholic civilization on the outskirts of Russian lands. Vilnius retained the borderline status in the 19th century, in the inter-war years and even in the time of Soviet occupation. Even today it is located not in the middle of the Republic of Lithuania, but in the east, approximately thirty kilometres away from the Belorussian border. Therefore, despite historical changes, Vilnius has always remained at the border, though the border itself kept moving. At the same time, Vilnius was – and is – a bridge between different cultural regions. The free democratic Lithuania faces a task of creating a new identity for Vilnius without rejecting a single historical and cultural streak of the city. Having integrated its entire past and its entire cultural potential, Vilnius is turning into a European capital worthy of its founders and best citizens.

1 Step fibula. Bronze. 7th–8th cent.  2 Amber amulets. 3rd mill. AD
3 Cross-shaped pin. 8th cent.  4 Amber amulet. 3rd mill. AD
5 Fibula.  4th–5th cent.  6 Horseshoe fibula. 4th–5th cent.
Opposite p.: The earliest known Lithuanian money – silver moulds. 12th–14th cent.

# Prehistoric times

The present territory of the city, the valleys of two not wide but swift rivers – the Neris and the Vilnia – have been inhabited since the Palaeolithic times. The cultural layer at the foot of the Vilnius Castle Hill, at the Old Arsenal, dates back to about the 4th mill. BC, and on the Castle Hill itself – to the 1st mill. BC, which implies that Vilnius equals Athens and Rome in age. Little can be said about earlier population, but probably since 2000–2500 BC they were Baltic (or Pre-Baltic) tribes. The Balts are a particular branch of Indo-Europeans, their languages are neither Slavonic nor Germanic; because of their particular archaism

linguists compare them to Sanskrit, Old Greek and Latin. Baltic mythology and customs are also unique. In prehistoric times the Balts inhabited a territory stretching from the lower Vistula almost to Kiev and Moscow, but this area gradually narrowed down. Only two small Baltic nations – Lithuanians and Latvians – have survived into our days, having successfully defended their identity from historical catastrophes and more powerful neighbours.

In the 5th cent. BC there was a sizeable settlement at the foot of the Castle Hill, through which trade routes led. However, creation of the Lithuanian state started as late as the 13th century. Its first outstanding ruler Mindaugas was baptized in 1251 and crowned King of Lithuania on July 6th 1253.

It is assumed that it was Mindaugas who built the first Cathedral in Vilnius. Traces of the original Cathedral incorporating Romanesque style features have been discovered in the vaults of the present Cathedral. Wooden buildings and remains of flooring from the same period have also been discovered. After Mindaugas' death the Christian Cathedral was probably turned into a place of pagan worship; however, the city remained an important centre of Eastern Lithuania, probably with some features of a capital.

1, 3 Medal commemorating the 600th anniversary of Vilnius. 1923. Art. P. Rimša
2 Gediminas is building the castle of Vilnius. 1882. Art. M.E. Andriolli

# The founding of the city

According to a legend recorded in the Chronicle of Lithuania, Vilnius was established by Gediminas, Grand Duke of Lithuania, who ruled the country ca. 70 years after Mindaugas and called himself "King of the Lithuanians and many Russians". The legend relates that he went hunting from his residence in Trakai, killed a huge aurochs and fell asleep in the Šventaragis valley at the foot of the present Castle Hill. In his dream he saw an iron wolf that howled like a hundred wolves. This prophetic dream was explained by the pagan priest Lizdeika. He told Gediminas that in this location he should build a castle and found a city that would be unconquerable like an iron wolf, and that the howling of a hundred wolves signified the glory of this city – it would resound in all countries of the world. That was what Gediminas did, naming the new city – his capital-to-be – after the Vilnia river.

This myth is reminiscent of the myth of the founding of Rome, where a central role is also assumed by a she-wolf. Both myths can possibly be derived from the same Indo-European archetype. Reality, of course, is somewhat different, since already in Gediminas' times a large settlement existed close to the Neris and the Vilnia. Legends also confirm the existence of a sacral centre; they say that since olden times deceased rulers used to be ritually burned in the Šventaragis valley (Šventaragis himself is one of these mythic dukes who, according to the legend, ruled after Mindaugas). One fact is evident: Gediminas transferred the capital from Trakai to Vilnius probably because it was easier for him to defend this place from enemy attacks, and probably because it was more convenient for trade. At that time Lithuania fought a two hundred-year war with Teutonic knights, who tried to convert the Lithuanians – "Northern Saracens" – with the sword.

On January 25th 1323 Gediminas sent a letter written in Latin from his new capital, stressing the fact that it was written "in our city of Vilnius". This date is considered the birthday of Vilnius. Gediminas wrote additional letters that are considered to be the earliest examples of Lithuanian writing. In these letters addressed to German cities – Magdeburg, Bremen, Köln and others, – and monasteries, Gediminas invited merchants, craftsmen and priests to Lithuania, and promised to guarantee them the same rights that were enjoyed by citizens of Riga (the present capital of Latvia, Riga, was founded by German conquerors as early as 1201). Besides, he mentioned the fact that in the pagan Vilnius there were two Catholic churches – Franciscan and Dominican. On October 2nd 1323 Gediminas signed a peace treaty with the city of Riga, its bishop and German knights, and in 1325 formed a union with King of Poland Ladislas the Cubit and married his daughter Aldona to Ladislas' son. In this way the Lithuanian state with the capital Vilnius became a recognized member of the community of European nations. Gediminas started a dynasty that was to rule Lithuania (and later, also Poland) for more than two hundred years;

1 Crossbow fibula. 10th–11th cent.  2 Swords. 10th–12th cent.
3 Remains of Gothic masonry on Šv. Ignoto St.  4 Broad-bladed battle axes. 11th–12th cent.
Opposite p.: The earliest parchment containing a reference to the territory of Lithuania – the letter
by the Grand Duke Jogaila of February 17th 1387 granting the Cathedral a domain

many noble Russian families descend from the Gediminas dynasty as well.

Of Gediminas' seven sons, the most famous were Algirdas and Kęstutis. They jointly ruled Lithuania. The first lived in Vilnius and ruled the eastern lands of the country, while the second resided in Trakai, west of the capital, and defended Lithuania from the Teutonic order. Period sources mention three Vilnius castles: the Higher, the Lower and the Crooked Castle. The Higher Castle on the Gediminas Hill was a fortress, the Lower Castle a residence of the Grand Duke, and the Crooked Castle (built of timber) most probably was situated on the present Hill of Three Crosses.

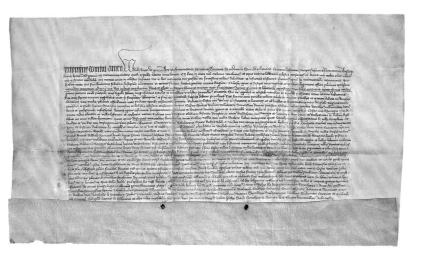

The brothers Algirdas and Kęstutis got along well, which cannot be said about Algirdas' son Jogaila and Kęstutis' son Vytautas. After Algirdas' death, Jogaila dethroned Kęstutis and imprisoned him together with his son in the castle of Krewo. Kęstutis died or was killed there, while Vytautas escaped and started a war against Jogaila. In this war he resorted to the help of the Teutonic order. The joint army of Vytautas and the Teutonic order attacked the city several times. A participant in the crucial attack in 1390 was Henry Bolingbroke who later became Henry IV, King of England (the character of Shakespeare's famous historical drama). In his words, at that time the city was built of wood and did not have defensive walls, but the castle was stone; the invaders burned down nearly the entire city and the Crooked Castle, but failed to seize the Higher Castle. Before long, in 1392, Vytautas made peace with Jogaila and took over Gediminas' throne becoming the Grand Duke of Lithuania. From that time on, he became the main adversary of the Teutonic knights; in 1394 and 1402 he forced their army to retreat from Vilnius, and after that the city enjoyed a period of peaceful development for two and a half centuries.

1, 2 Coin of the Grand Duke of Lithuania Jogaila. Late 14th cent.
3 Coin of the Grand Duke of Lithuania Vytautas. 14th cent.
4 Grand Duke of Lithuania Vytautas (ca. 1350–1430). From the album of J. Matejko
5 Pipe – kalian. 2nd half of the 19th cent.  6 Mass at the Tartar mosque.  1785–86. Art. F. Smuglewicz
7 Karaite woman's cap. 19th cent.  8 Tablecloth – kichata. 19th cent.

# Lithuania's Christianization
## and the growth of the city

The wars of Jogaila and Vytautas coincided with great changes in Lithuania's state life and culture. In 1385 Jogaila signed the so-called Krewo Union. According to this union, Jogaila had to marry a young Polish princess Jadwiga, christen Lithuania and unite both states. In 1387 Jogaila destroyed a pagan temple in Vilnius, extinguished the holy fire, re-established a bishopric and built a cathedral. In the same year Vilnius was granted the right of self-government (so-called Magdeburg right), though its rudiments must have existed earlier. Having become the king of Poland (under the name of Władysław Jagiełło), Jogaila moved to Krakow, while Vilnius saw the beginning of Vytautas' era.

In Vytautas' times Vilnius became increasingly multi-national. Since Gediminas' times Germans and Eastern Slavs – Ruthenians – lived in their own communities and had temples in Vilnius. Both communities settled in the suburbs, while inhabitants of the so-called inner city were local people. In the Lukiškės suburb Vytautas settled Tartar captives and granted them certain privileges, while Trakai became home to Karaites whom he had brought along from the Crimea (they settled in Vilnius as well). At about the same time the Jewish community started to grow in the capital, later to become its distinct and inseparable part.

The Flemish traveller Ghillebert de Lannoy who visited Vilnius in 1414 was the first to give a more extensive description of the city. According to him, there was a castle on the hill (its remains are still there), Vytautas' palace stood in the castle courtyard, and a long and narrow city, mainly wooden, with several stone churches, sloped down from another more distant hill towards the castle. It is known that at that time there were two market squares in Vilnius, a smaller one at St. John's Church, and a larger one in the place where the Town Hall was later built. Originally pavements were wood planking, but in Vytautas' times many streets were stone-paved. Brick houses, particularly noblemen's residencies, appeared.

Vytautas' brother Sigismund who ruled briefly after his brother's death in 1430, granted equal rights to the capital's Russian Orthodox believers – before long they came to constitute one half of the members of the city board and guild elders. The so-called chancellery Slavonic language played an important role in the culture of Vilnius and Lithuania. Used in the chancellery of the Grand Duke, it was also the language of the Lithuanian chronicles and the famous code of the period law – the Statute of Lithuania. It was not until the 16th cent. that the Lithuanian language acquired a written form, though for many – probably even the majority – city residents it was the native tongue. It is interesting to note that the observation of a semblance of Lithuanian to Latin led to the advancement of a project to proclaim Latin the state language. This project failed, as the Lithuanian aristocracy and the Grand Duke's court itself

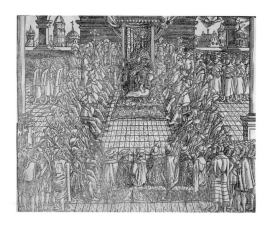

1 Nicholas of Cusa. Improved map of Central Europe (Vilnius is marked here for the first time).
From the atlas *Geographia* by Ptolemy. Strasbourg, 1513
2 Royal seal of Sigismund of the Kęstutis dynasty (ca. 1365–1440)
3 View of the parliament hall of Alexander Jagiellon. 1619

rapidly became Polonized. It should be noted that in the old city of Vilnius there are German, Russian, Jewish and Tartar streets, but Lithuanian or Polish streets do not exist – these two nations have never been regarded as minorities. Having switched to the Polish language, local noblemen still considered themselves Lithuanians and often were rather hostile to indigenous Polish lands (the so-called Polish Crown). This situation persisted until the 19th and even 20th cent., becoming a source of numerous paradoxes.

In 1440, Jogaila's son Casimir became the Grand Duke of Lithuania (four years later also the King of Poland). Though his son Prince Casimir never became a ruler, he surpassed his father. He was expected to ascend the throne of Hungary, but the elected Hungarian king Matthew Corvinus succeeded in blocking him. Pious and physically weak since childhood, the young Casimir led a spiritual life and in 1484 died of tuberculosis at the age of 25. His remains in the Vilnius Cathedral won fame for miracles, and in 1604 Casimir was elevated to the sainthood. He is considered the patron saint of Lithuania and Poland. The cult of St. Casimir left a deep mark in the history and art of Lithuania. This saint of Vilnius is worshipped also far away from Lithuania, for example, in Latin America.

The father of St. Casimir, Casimir Jagiellon, ruled Lithuania for 52 years. These years were extremely favourable for Vilnius that enjoyed a quiet and peaceful life, expanding alongside the Neris banks and slowly turning into a city built of brick. The Grand Duke renewed its Magdeburg privileges. According to these privileges, the city was administered by a senior and the magistrate court consisting of 12 burgomasters and 24 councillors. However, not the entire city was subject to the citizens' self-government. Since olden times a part of it was administered by the castle elder, another part by the bishop; later other jurisdictions appeared, e.g. assigned to monasteries. Decrees and the court's decisions were pronounced in Lithuanian, Polish, sometimes in German and also in the language of Eastern Slavs – Ruthenians. Vilnius was the seat of the Lithuanian Seimas and the noblemen's council. In 1489 a mint started to operate. Markets used to be held on a weekly basis; in addition, Casimir granted rights for two large fortnight fairs – after the Epiphany and the Feast of the Assumption.

The Grand Duke of Lithuania and King of Poland Alexander Jagiellon (1492–1506) preferred Vilnius to Krakow; he was the only ruler of the Lithuanian-Polish state to be buried in the Vilnius Cathedral. In his times Vilnius became one of the major European cities. Alexander built a new stone Lower Castle, established the Arsenal and set up a pharmacy; he had the Vilnius Town Hall rebuilt, and citizens were ordered to build a stone wall surrounding the capital (Vilnius was threatened by Tartars' attacks). In 1495 craftsmen – goldsmiths and tailors – established their first guilds in Vilnius; soon the number of guilds reached 20 (before that the sole citizens' organizations were so-called mead fraternities).

1 Francis Skoryna (before 1490–before 1541)
2 Bona Sforza (1494–1557). From the album of J. Matejko
3 Nicholas Radziwiłł (1470–1522), Vilnius voivode and the Chancellor of the Grand Duchy. 16th cent.
4 Sigismund the Old (1506–48). Ca. 1548  5 Mikalojus Daukša. *Catechism.* 1595
Opposite p.: 1, 2 Choral psalm (antiphon) books. 14th cent.
3 Statute of Lithuania in Polish, published in Vilnius in 1614

# The Renaissance era

The rule of Jogaila's two last descendants: Sigismund the Old (1506–48) and Sigis-mund Augustus (1548–72) is considered the golden age of Vilnius. At that time the city became a Renaissance capital of European stature, competing with Florence or Milan. This happened largely due to the fact that Sigismund the Old married the Italian princess Bona Sforza, who brought along a sizeable Italian community that settled in Vilnius. Queen Bona introduced the customs of her homeland, from Italian music and cuisine to the art of political intrigues. It was at that time when Vilnius architecture acquired the Italian tinge that has survived into our days.

Since the capital was regularly devastated by fires that would damage both the castle and the Cathedral, Sigismund the Old had a water supply system

 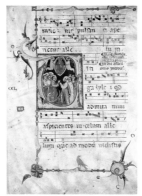 

installed in Vilnius. In 1536 the first bridge over the Neris, later called Žaliasis (Green), was built (it has remained in its original place). A paper factory (1527), a glass workshop (1547), a cannon foundry and two hospitals were established in Vilnius. In 1522 the first printing house was put into operation; its founder was Francis Skoryna, the father of Belorussian literature, who published *The Small Travel Book* and *The Apostle* there. Somewhat later two more printing houses – Latin and Polish – (1533) appeared, but the first Lithuanian book in Vilnius had to wait until 1595: it was a Catholic *Catechism* published by Mikalojus Daukša (until that time only books of the Lithuanian Reformers were published in Eastern Prussia). Curiously enough, the first Latvian book also came out in Vilnius and even earlier than Lithuanian (1585).

The competition between the Reformers and Catholics had a significant influence on the development of the city. In 1539 the famous Lithuanian Reformer Abraomas Kulvietis, a pupil of Luther and Melanchton, founded a school in Vilnius. Three years later it was closed down and Kulvietis himself had to flee to Koenigsberg. However, in 1555 the first Evangelical church was built in Vilnius. A number of Lithuanian noblemen, among them many repre-

1, 2 Medal of Nicholas Radziwiłł the Black (1515–65),
Chancellor of the Grand Duchy and Vilnius voivode. 1563
3 Barbora Radvilaitė (ca. 1520–51)
4 Sigismund August (1520–72). Engraving from the publication
*Statuta y przywileie...* by Jan Herbort. Krakow, 1570
5 Map of Central Europe. From the atlas *Cosmographia Universalis* by S. Münster. Basel, 1572
Opposite p.: Portrait-tiles from the Lower Castle of Vilnius. 16th cent.

sentatives of the Radziwiłł family, embraced the Reformation. In 1563 the
Vilnius Seimas proclaimed freedom for all religious denominations. At that
time Lithuania became the most important centre of tolerance and liberalism in
Europe. The Counter-Reformation took over as late as the 17th cent., and
Lithuania remained a predominantly Catholic country. However, in Vilnius
there still are temples of both Evangelical Lutherans and Reformers.

In 1529 the Statute of Lithuania, one of the most significant period legal codes
in Europe, was adopted in Vilnius; its revised editions appeared in 1566 and 1588.

In the era of Sigismund the Old (1522) the construction of the Vilnius defensive wall was completed. Half stone and half timber, it surrounded the city with
a perimeter of ca. 3 km, its height was 12 m, and the thickness – 2–3 m. Starting at
the Lower Castle, the wall followed the present Liejyklos, Pylimo, Šv. Dvasios and

Bokšto streets and reached the Vilnia, whose steep slopes protected the city from
the east. The wall had 9 gates and several towers. The most powerful gate, a
real mediaeval fortress, was the Subačius Gate, and the most famous one –
Medininkai, or the Gate of Dawn. The area of the city within the wall, excluding
the castle, totalled 85 ha. On the other side of the wall stretched the suburbs –
Užupis and Lukiškės (built perhaps already in the 14th cent.), Rasos and Antakalnis (known since the 15th cent.). The wall survived until the early 19th cent.:
in 1800–05 it was pulled down by the Russian occupational authorities. Only
the Gate of Dawn and small fragments of the wall in several places remained.

During the rule of Sigismund Augustus Vilnius reached its peak of pros-
perity. This last representative of the Jagellonian dynasty established his court
mainly in Vilnius instead of Krakow – first as a vicegerent of his father,
Sigismund the Old, and later also as King of Poland. He was particularly
attached to Vilnius because of a love affair that has become another romantic
myth of the city: the king fell in love and married the widowed local beauty
Barbora Radvilaitė (Barbara Radziwiłł), though Polish noblemen refused to recognize this unequal marriage for quite a long time. Barbora died early
(rumours went that she was poisoned by her mother-in-law Bona Sforza). The
vaults of the Vilnius Cathedral hold a sarcophagus of this ill-fated queen.

Sigismund Augustus rebuilt the Lower Castle and furnished it in a very luxurious style. It was turned into a centre of Renaissance culture, boasting an

1 The Old Town Hall of Vilnius in the 2nd half of the 18th cent. After P. Rossi's drawing
2 Piotr Skarga (1530–91), the first rector of the Vilnius Academy. 17th cent.
3 Vilnius Bishop Walerian Protasewicz (1504–79), the initiator of founding the Vilnius Collegium
4 The Great Synagogue of Vilnius. 1785–86. Art. P. Smuglevičius
Opposite p.: The first known layout of Vilnius
from the atlas *Cities of the World...* by G. Braun. Vol. 3. 1576

excellent library (later it became the property of Vilnius University), a theatre, a choir, a picture gallery, and a collection of tapestries. The castle, as well as other venues of the city, were open for masquerades and competitions, scholarly disputes and feasts. In Vilnius the ruler kept horse-stables with two thousand horses and even something like a zoo – five bears, a lion and ten camels. The post route Vilnius–Krakow–Vienna–Venice, opened in 1562, symbolized a firm link between Lithuania and Western Europe.

Noblemen were eager to keep up with their ruler. In the time of Sigismund Augustus and later, magnate families like the Radziwiłłs, Sapiehas, Chodkiewiczes, Kiszkas and others erected luxurious residencies. In the 16th

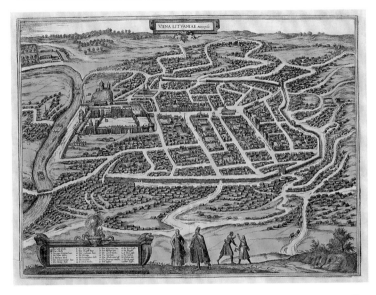

cent. two and three storey brick houses must have prevailed; a new town hall, many churches and monasteries were built. Many picturesque Vilnius lanes have survived from that period. Particularly famous were the city gardens that stretched mostly alongside the Neris banks. Sigismund Augustus granted a nobleman's status to the members of the magistrate and their descendants. The number of German, Czech and other craftsmen increased. The Jewish community (kahal) lived under its separate jurisdiction. Under Sigismund Augustus the part of the city inhabited by the Jews occupied a large area between the present Didžioji, Pylimo and Dominikonų streets. A synagogue in Vilnius is known since 1572, though Judaic prayer houses must have existed earlier. It is not known exactly when the first Jews appeared in Vilnius (some think that in Vytautas' or even Gediminas' times), but their community gradually became the most influential and active Israelite diaspora since the times of Babylon and mediaeval Cordoba, and Vilnius – the most prominent centre of Judaism in the world replacing the Rhine land. Despite the Jews' religious isolation, they acted

1, 2 Sigismund August gold ten-ducat coin. Vilnius mint. 1562
3 Military leader Caspar Bekesh (1520–1579). Middle of the 19th cent. Art. J. Ozębłowski
4 Stephen Batory (1533–86). 17th cent.
5 Seal of Vilnius Tailors' Guild. 16th–17th cent.
Opposite p.: Medal of Vilnius Bishop Eustachy Wołłowicz (ca. 1560–1630). 1626

as intermediaries between Lithuania and Europe, while the local law and politics of the majority of dukes allowed them to live peacefully in a gentile environment.

On July 1st 1569 the Lublin union joined Lithuania and Poland into one state with an elected monarch. Vilnius became a secondary city: elected rulers, though still called grand dukes of Lithuania, did not consider it the second capital of the state and visited it on rare occasions. An exception was the elected king Stephen Batory, a Hungarian. However, under the patronage of prominent voivodes from the Chodkiewicz, Sapieha and other families, the city remained lively and prosperous. It continued to trade with Poland, Prussia, Hungary, Moscow and even the Oriental countries. The wave of Counter-Reformation brought to Vilnius the Jesuit order that made a great contribution to Lithuanian education: in 1570 Jesuits founded a school of higher education (college), which was promoted to the status of an academy by King Stephen Batory in 1579. On

October 29th of the same year Pope Gregory XII issued a bull acknowledging the Vilnius Academy as a university.

The University became the major intellectual centre of Vilnius and Lithuania, and remains such until our days. It is regarded as one of the oldest and most respectable universities in Eastern and Central Europe, succeeding the universities of Prague, Krakow, Pécs and Koenigsberg in terms of age. In the 16th cent. and even later Vilnius University played an exceptional role as the Eastern European scholarly centre influencing not only ethnic Lithuania and the multi-lingual and multi-confessional Grand Duchy of Lithuania, but also the neighbouring lands. At that time it was important to all Catholic Europe and occupied a special place in the development of the world's philosophical thought.

 Prominent professors of the old Vilnius Academy included: philosopher Martynas Smigleckis (Marcin Smiglecki), poet Motiejus Kazimieras Sarbievijus (Maciej Kazimierz Sarbiewski), historian Albertas Kojalavičius-Vijūkas, rhetorician and musician Žygimantas Liauksminas, writer and linguist Konstantinas Sirvydas, mathematician and engineer Osvald Krüger; among students of the university were the author of the first Russian grammar Meletii Smotrycki, the

ANDRE. SNIADECKI.

1 Konstantinas Sirvydas (1579–1631). 17th cent.
2 Martynas Počobutas (1728–1810). Early 19th cent. Art. J. Damelis
3 Jędrzej Śniadecki (1768–1838)  4 Jan Śniadecki (1756–1830)
5 Motiejus Kazimieras Sarbievijus (1595–1640)
Opposite p.: Vilnius with the city wall in the 16th–17th cent.
Engravings and lithograph from *Album de Wilna* by Jan Kazimierz Wilczyński

founder of the rocket theory Kazimieras Simonavičius (Kazimierz Sie-
menowicz), the Catholic saint Andrew Bobola tortured to death by Cossacks. In
the 18th–19th cent. the secularized university was made famous by the
astronomer Martynas Počobutas (Marcin Poczobutt), botanist Stanislovas
Bonifacas Jundzilas (Stanisław Bonifacy Jundziłł), natural scientist Johann
Georg Forster who took part in James Cook's expedition, mathematician and
philosopher Jan Śniadecki, his brother chemist Jędrzej Śniadecki and many others. Courtyards and halls of the university still recall the great Polish poets
Adam Mickiewicz and Juliusz Słowacki and the father of the Lithuanian
national revival movement Simonas Daukantas. In the 20th cent. many
European level scholars worked in the Polish Stephen Batory University and

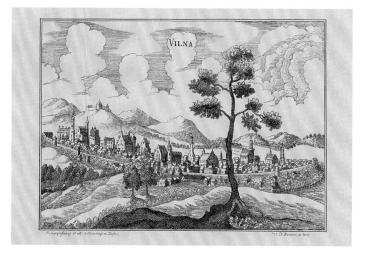

the Lithuanian University; it was there that specialists in many fields, numerous writers, thinkers and contributors to the restoration of Lithuania's independence received their education.

Though the university was a stronghold of the Jesuit Counter-Reformation,
its collegium and the philosophical faculty remained open also to Reformers
and Russian Orthodox believers (only the theological faculty was purely
Catholic). It was not until the 17th cent. that this spirit of tolerance faded away.
Both professor and student communities were international. Professors' lists,
alongside Lithuanians, Poles, Russians, Belorussians and Ukrainians, include
German, English, Scottish, Irish, Swedish, Norwegian, Spanish and Portuguese
names. Among the students were even Finns and Tartars. While visiting Vilnius
in 1648, King Ladislas Vasa was greeted in 18 languages at the university,
among them Lithuanian, Polish, Ruthenian and, of course, the language of
teaching, Latin.

The extensive Latin literature of the Grand Duchy, an integral part of its cultural legacy, was also related to the university. Epic poems, elegies, eulogies,

1 Mikalojus Daukša. *Postilla*. Printing house of the Vilnius Academy, 1599
2 *The Seven Chodkiewicz Heroes*. Printing house of the Vilnius Academy, 1642
3 Albertas Kojalavičius-Vijūkas. *History of Lithuania* Vol. 1. Danzig, 1650
4 *Lyricorum libri tres* by Motiejus Kazimieras Sarbievijus. 4th edition. Antwerp, 1632.
Engraving after Peter Paul Rubens' drawing
Opposite p.:
Kazimieras Simonavičius. *The Great Artillery Art*. Amsterdam, 1650
Michalonis Lituani. *On the Customs of the Tartars, Lithuanians and Muscovites*. Basel, 1615
Nicholas Christopher Radziwiłł the Orphan. *A Journey to Jerusalem*. Braniev, 1601

epitaphs, satires, epigrams, rhetoric speeches, historical treatises and various "literary games" were composed in Vilnius. Authors represented the Lithuanian environment in the style of Horace, Ovid and Titus Livius, the Gediminas Castle was transposed into the Capitolium, and the residents of Vilnius became Romans. Alongside Latin texts, literary works were also created in local languages. The first rector of the university Piotr Skarga was a famous Polish preacher, the second Jakub Wujek – a translator of the Bible into Polish. Motiejus Strijkovskis (Maciej Stryjkowski), related with Vilnius in many ways, wrote the first history of Lithuania in Polish. The city councillor, Calvinist Daniel Naborowski (who might have studied in Padua with Galileo) created excellent Polish baroque poems, often compared with examples of

English metaphysical poetry. Mikalojus Daukša published in Vilnius the translation of Wujek's *Postilla*, a significant monument of the Lithuanian language, and the university professor Konstantinas Sirvydas wrote a book of sermons in Lithuanian.

Typically of Vilnius, nearly all the writers mentioned above were multi-lingual. For example, Daukša wrote a foreword to his translation of the *Postilla*, which is regarded as a Renaissance manifesto confirming the rights of the Lithuanian language; however, the foreword is written in Polish. Sirvydas himself used to translate his sermons into Polish. On the other hand, Stryjkowski's history includes some texts in Lithuanian, while Naborowski in one of his Polish poems plays with the Lithuanian word "verkti" ("to cry"). Multi-lingualism remained a trait of the Vilnius culture until the 17th and even 18th cent.: e.g. Jesuits used to stage Polish dramas with inserted Lithuanian episodes. But in the 18th cent. the Lithuanian language was demoted to the secondary status with regard to Polish. A special written form of Lithuanian was developed, where only the basic grammar remained Lithuanian, but almost the entire vocabulary was assimilated from Polish. This form was discarded only at the time of Lithuanian national revival, at the end of the 19th cent.

1 The Miracle by St. Casimir's Coffin. 1848. From *Album de Wilna* by Jan Kazimierz Wilczyński
2 Michael Casimir Pac (ca. 1624–82). 1691
3 Sigismund Vasa (1566–1632). After 1624. Workshop of Peter Paul Rubens
4 Gaon of Vilnius – Eliah ben Solomon Zalman (1720–97)  5 Hoard from the 16th–middle of the 18th cent.
Opposite p.: Fire in Vilnius. Detail of the engraving from the 2nd half of the 18th cent.

# The 17th century

The period following Stephen Batory's rule was marked by a gradual decline of Vilnius. Even the city's population shrunk. Noblemen took over entire city blocks and looked down on ordinary citizens, limited the rights of the magistrates, guilds and merchants' corporations. Quarrels among the magnates sometimes turned into limited internal wars. In 1611–39 fierce battles between Catholics and Reformers broke out. Vilnius was devastated by fires: on July 1st 1610 the castle, the Cathedral, 17 Catholic and 3 Evangelical churches, the university and almost 5,000 houses were destroyed by fire. True, in the end this proved to be an advantage for the city: excellent monuments of early Baroque, such as the Churches of St. Casimir and St. Theresa, were built, the Church of St. Michael was completed, and a chapel in the Cathedral holding the remains of the Lithuanian patron saint St. Casimir was set up after the fire. The Vilnius silhouette turned Baroque with vibrant domes and towers.

Under King Ladislas Vasa's rule, theatre flourished in Vilnius. Already in the 16th cent. Italian and English actors used to come to Vilnius on tours, but it

was Ladislas Vasa who set up a permanent court theatre (1632–48) with opera, ballet and comedy companies and invited guest artists from Venice, Rome and Paris. In 1636 the first Italian opera *The Abduction of Helen* was produced in Vilnius.

In the middle of the 17th cent. the Lithuanian capital suffered a hard blow from a war with the Moscow tsar Aleksei Mikhailovich, the father of Peter the Great. The Moscow army invaded the city on August 8th 1655 – it was the first time since the Teutonic knights' attacks that Vilnius was seized by enemies. More than ten thousand Vilnius residents were killed, fire raged for 17 days, much wealth was plundered and destroyed. Vilnius remained under the Russian rule for 5 years. In 1660 it was liberated by hetman Michael Casimir Pac, but a garrison of Muscovites were besieged in the Higher Castle until 1661. To commemorate these events Pac built the most remarkable baroque monument in Vilnius – the Church of St. Peter and St. Paul (1668–76), and in the Verkiai suburb, so-called Calvary chapels were erected.

The role of the Jewish community gained importance, though the tolerance of Sigismund Augustus's times was not maintained. The Jews engaged in commerce and crafts. In 1633 Ladislas Vasa ordered the Jews to live separately from Christians, in a ghetto (the boundaries of the ghetto approximately coincided

1 Pranciškus Smuglevičius (1745–1807). Self-portrait
2 Stanislaus August Poniatowski (1732–98)
3 Laurynas Stuoka-Gucevičius (1753–98). 1823. Art. J.H. Głowacki
4 Jonas Rustemas (1762–1835). Self-portrait with a fez. After 1813
5 Medal commemorating the 100th anniversary of death of Tadeusz Kościuszko. 1917. Art. K. Łaszczka

with the area formerly inhabited by the Jews). Some of them settled in other parts of the city even after Ladislas Vasa's order, and the ghetto itself came into daily contact with the gentile environment. Jews knew the local languages, and in Vilnius University, like in other European universities, Hebrew was taught alongside Greek and Latin.

One of the most prominent Jewish spiritual leaders, Gaon Elijah (1720–97) was active in Vilnius; in Lithuania his Orthodox views prevailed against another mystical tradition of Judaism – Chasidism (Chasidic teachings were spread in the Western Ukraine).

# Partitions of the Commonwealth of Both Nations

In the 18th cent. the Lithuanian-Polish Commonwealth entered the last stage of its existence. At the beginning of the century it was ravaged by the so-called Northern war. Several times Vilnius was occupied by Swedish and Russian armies – they plundered the city and burdened it with heavy contributions. The Russian tsar Peter the Great, an ally of the King of Poland August II, stayed in Vilnius for 6 weeks (1705). According to a legend, in Vilnius he baptized an African boy Hannibal, the great-grandfather of the famous Russian poet Alexander Pushkin.

In the second half of the 18th cent. the first Vilnius newspaper appeared – the Polish weekly *Kurier Litewski* (The Lithuanian Courier, 1760–63), later replaced by *Gazety Wileńskie* (Vilnius Newspapers, 1764–93).

In the time of the last king Stanislaus August Poniatowski (1764–95) in Vilnius, as in the entire Commonwealth, Enlightenment ideas and radical social concepts gained ground. In 1773, after the Jesuit order had been banished, Vilnius University was transferred to the state's jurisdiction, which for that purpose established the so-called Educational Commission – the first Ministry of Education in Europe. In 1781 the university was renamed as the Chief School of the Grand Duchy of Lithuania. Many secular scholars of European stature worked there. Established already in the Jesuit era, the astronomical observatory was renewed in 1782–88 and competed with the Greenwich and Paris observatories. Another famous school related to the university was the Vilnius Art School, whose members were the painters Pranciškus Smuglevičius (Franciszek Smuglewicz) and Jonas Rustemas (Jan Rustem), as well as the architect Laurynas Stuoka-Gucevičius (Wawrzyniec Gucewicz), who brought to Vilnius the spirit of French Classicism. He rebuilt the Vilnius Town hall (1785–99) and the Cathedral (1783–1801; reconstruction was finished after Stuoka-Gucevičius' death). These buildings of Vilnius are excellent examples of architecture nurtured by the ideas of the French revolution.

New moods pervaded the Vilnius City Theatre, founded in 1785 by the famous Polish actor, director and dramatist Wojciech Bogusławski. He famil-

1 Map of the Vilnius province. 19th cent.
2 Jakub Jasiński (1759 or 1761–94). From *Album de Wilna* by Jan Kazimierz Wilczyński
3 Cartoon of the first partition of the Commonwealth of Both Nations
4 Front page of the weekly *Kurier Litewski*. May 20th 1763
5 Medallion with a portrait of Tadeusz Kościuszko (1746–1817)

iarized Vilnius residents with the works of Molière, Voltaire, Beaumarchais, Lessing, Schiller and local authors. The theatre existed for more than 80 years – in 1866 it was closed by the Russian occupational authorities.

In 1772 Russia, Prussia and Austria annexed large regions of the Commonwealth – this was the first partition of Lithuania and Poland, followed by another one in 1793. Educators and radical politicians tried to save the shrinking endangered state: following the pattern of the American and French revolutions, they made haste to introduce basic reforms. The second partition brought about an uprising against the occupiers led by Tadeusz Kościuszko, who had distinguished himself as a brother-in-arms of George Washington in the American Independence War. The rebels issued a proclamation in Polish and Lithuanian, though at that time Vilnius was occupied by the Russian army. On April 24th, 1794 battles broke out once more. The leader was Jakub Jasiński; Laurynas Stuoka-Gucevičius was among the rebels. The entire Russian garrison was taken captive except the artillery that shelled the city from the western hills. However, it was too late to save Vilnius and the Commonwealth. The city remained free only until August 12th. Then the Russian army fought off the rebels defending the walls of Vilnius and seized it again. In 1795 the third partition of the Commonwealth completed the destruction of the state; Lithuania and Vilnius fell under Russia's occupation that lasted 120 years.

From the capital of an independent country Vilnius turned into a provincial city on the outskirts of the empire, the seat of the governor general and governor. The tsarist authorities cancelled its Magdeburg rights: in 1808 the magistrate was replaced by the city Duma subject to the province's administrative board. The census held in 1795 by the new authorities found in Vilnius as few as 17,690 inhabitants, among them 2,471 noblemen, 568 Catholic priests and 107 priests of other confessions, 238 teachers and professors, and 860 craftsmen in 38 guilds. There were 32 Catholic churches, 15 monasteries, 5 Uniate churches with 3 monasteries, one Russian Orthodox, one Lutheran and one Reformers' temple, and 10 noblemen's palaces.

The occupation went through several different stages. At first the pressure of the empire did not seem too heavy. After the death of tsarina Catherine II who destroyed the Commonwealth of Both Nations, her son Paul I released Tadeusz Kościuszko from prison. The son of Paul I, Alexander I seemed well-educated and liberal: the beginning of his rule raised hopes that the fate of Lithuania and Poland, and maybe even Russia itself, might take a turn for the better. In 1803 the Chief School was renamed as the Vilnius Imperial University. The tsar granted it a European-like statute that became an example for other universities of the Russian Empire. In 1811 the city's population was ca. 56,000 inhabitants: it ranked third in the empire after St. Petersburg and Moscow. This period saw the beginning of the second golden age in Vilnius: though quite short – less than thirty years, – it left an indelible trace in its culture.

1, 2 Medal for the seizure of Vilnius in 1812 with Napoleon's image
2 The retreating French army in the Town Hall Square in 1812.
From *Album de Wilna* by Jan Kazimierz Wilczyński
3 Medal commemorating the 100th anniversary of birth of Alexander I (1777–1825)
Opposite p.: Palace of the Governor General and the Astronomical Observatory of Vilnius
University in the 19th cent. From *Album de Wilna* by Jan Kazimierz Wilczyński

# Napoleon's war

A separate page in the history of Vilnius is Russia's war with Napoleon. On June 24–25th, 1812 a large army of the French emperor – 600,000 soldiers with 1,400 guns – crossed the Nemunas (this river marked the boundary of the Russian empire) and seized Kaunas. Alexander I learned the news at a feast that he was giving in the Vingis Park in Vilnius. The Russians retreated from the city having burned the Green Bridge. Attempts to make peace with Napoleon, – incidentally, described in Leo Tolstoy's *War and Peace*, – turned out to be unsuccessful. On June 28th the French army marched into Vilnius: Napoleon settled in the Bishops' Palace (now the Presidential Palace) for 19

days. There he held talks with local noblemen who hoped that this invasion would enable them to restore the independent republic of Lithuania and Poland, and established a provisional government (commission) led by Stanisław Soltan. However, Napoleon's promises were rather hollow. Having marched from Vilnius to Russia, he seized Moscow, but soon had to withdraw his army. Having lost the war, he reappeared in Vilnius in early December and before long retreated to Western Europe.

The catastrophe of Napoleon's Great Army, frozen and famished French soldiers that inundated the city's squares and streets, remained in the memory of the inhabitants of Vilnius for a long time. About 80,000 Frenchmen were buried in Vilnius (of Napoleon's army, as few as 20,000 soldiers remained). Together with the French army an officer Henri Beyle came to Vilnius; later he won world fame under the pseudonym of Stendhal and provided an excellent depiction of Napoleon's final defeat in his novel *The Charterhouse of Parma*. Stendhal put up at the house of the medical professor Józef Frank on Didžioji Street (now the French Culture Centre).

1 Johann Peter Frank ( 1745–1821). Art. A. Forstner
2 Joachim Lelewel (1786–1861). Art. J. Mackiewicz
3 Simonas Daukantas (1793–1864). 1850. Art. J. Zenkiewicz
4 Adam Mickiewicz (1799–1855). 1897. Art. S. Cheymann
5 Glass with engraved Freemason symbols and inscription "1817 Teodor Narbutt"
6, 7 Goblet and symbol of "The Zealous Lithuanian" mason lodge. 19th cent.

# Under tsars' rule

After the 1812 war Vilnius enjoyed several years of quite peaceful and almost happy life. These years were particularly favourable for the university, which succeeded in attracting famous educators – the brothers Śniadecki, Joachim Lelewel, Leon Borowski, Ignacy Daniłowicz and others. Well-known societies of medical doctors and physicists were active at the university. Polish replaced Latin as the language of teaching, though the latter was still used for writing theses; however, Lithuanian-speaking students were quite numerous – they seem to have had an informal society. Quite a few famous Vilnius residents belonged to the Masonic society: their rituals served as a cover for the liberal and often quite radical thought. Several newspapers were published, the most interesting of which was *Wiadomości Brukowe* (Street News) published by the Szubrawcy, or Rascals, society, whose goal was "to mend corrupted customs with laughter".

It was at that time when Polish Romanticism, often also called Polish-Lithuanian Romanticism, was born in Vilnius. The work of the great Romantic poets Adam Mickiewicz and Juliusz Słowacki is an important part of European and world literature; it is dear to all Vilnius residents, whatever language they may speak and whatever tradition they may belong to.

Both Adam Mickiewicz and Juliusz Słowacki studied at Vilnius University. Mickiewicz became involved in a clandestine students' circle, the so-called Philomatic Society (1817), whose members were Tomasz Zan, Jan Czeczot and others. Somewhat later the Philomats were joined by the societies of "the Radiant" and Philarets. Patterned after the Masonic lodges, in their statutes they declared the nurturing of science and morals, but the tsarist authorities had a good reason to suspect that their goal in fact was the restoration of independence. In 1823 the most prominent members of these societies, Mickiewicz among them, were arrested, imprisoned in the Basilian Monastery in Vilnius and after some time deported to Russia. All these events were later described by Mickiewicz in his drama *The Forefathers' Eve*, one of the major works of Polish literature.

The fathers of the Lithuanian revival movement – Simonas Stanevičius and particularly Simonas Daukantas – had also studied at Vilnius University. They were contemporaries of Mickiewicz and Słowacki (Daukantas might have known Mickiewicz and was even considered a candidate to the Philarets), but took a different path and ventured to write in the "peasant" Baltic language that Polish Romantic poets considered to be doomed to disappear. The Lithuanian intelligentsia of peasant origins that emerged in the 2nd half of the 19th cent. continued the work of Daukantas and Stanevičius creating the Lithuanian press, literature, culture, in other words – the Lithuanian national identity. The "philological revolution" that they carried out changed the face and image of the country. The Lithuanian national revival movement was accompanied by the Belorussian one that was partly modelled on the former. One of its founders was a friend of Mickiewicz, Philomat Jan Czeczot.

1 Konstanty Kalinowski (1838–64). Photo by A. Bonoldi  2 Mikhail Muravyov (1786–1866)
3 Zygmunt Sierakowski (1826–63) in prison. 1863. Etching by B. Zalecki
4 Demolition of the Church of St. Joseph the Betrothed. 1872–74. Photo by J. Czechowicz
5 Silver goblet with the coat of arms of the 1831 uprising  6 Coat of arms of the 1863 insurgents
Opposite p.: Mikhail Muravyov (in the centre) with officials. 1860's.

The Romantic era is associated with two unsuccessful uprisings against the tsarist authorities that had a painful effect on Vilnius. The first uprising that started in Warsaw in November 1830, reached Lithuania in the spring of 1831. On June 19th of that year, on Paneriai hills near Vilnius, a battle took place, in which the general of the rebels Antoni Giełgud was defeated. Having crushed the uprising, in 1832 the Russian authorities closed down the source of "dangerous attitudes" – Vilnius University. They left only the faculties of medicine and theology, called the Surgical and Spiritual Academies, but before long these faculties were transferred from Vilnius elsewhere. In 1839 the Uniates were made to convert to Russian Orthodoxy, and in 1840 the Statute of Lithuania was cancelled.

January 1863 brought a new uprising that acquired a very serious character in Lithuania. On February 1st, the rebels' committee of the Lithuanian province

proclaimed itself a revolutionary government and issued a manifesto, which, among other things, promised to give land to peasants. The uprising was led by Zygmunt Sierakowski (Zigmas Sierakauskas), Konstanty Kalinowski (Kostas Kalinauskas or Kastus Kalinouski), and Antanas Mackevičius. As these names reveal, the participants of the struggle were Lithuanians, Poles and Belorussians – many of them could have hardly told to which ethnic group they belonged. It was the last historic moment when the nations of the former Commonwealth marched together in the hope of restoring the former state (even if some of them cherished a goal of building several different states).

The uprising was mercilessly suppressed by Governor General Mikhail Muravyov nicknamed the Hanger, sent by the tsar Alexander II. Having established the Special Interrogation Committee, he sentenced to death many leaders of the rebels: Sierakowski and Kalinowski were hanged in the Lukiškės Square in Vilnius, and Mackevičius – in Kaunas. All in all, 37 patriots were executed in Vilnius, and many more were deported to Siberia. Severe repressive actions were followed by Russification. Even the name of Lithuania disappeared from the official press – it was called the North Western region. The Lithuanian press in Latin

1 The Vileišis brothers (from left to right): Jonas, Petras, Antanas, Anupras.
1904. Photo by B. Medzionis

2 Plaque with the Vytis emblem from Pilies Bridge across the Vilnia,
cast in the Vileišis metal works. Ca. 1900

3 Badge of the district elder of the Vilnius province

4 Tower of the Higher Castle 1906. Photo by L. and M. Butkowski

5 Badge of an agent of the Vilnius city board. 1892  6 Label of an atelier of hats. Early 20th cent.

Opposite p.: Sewage installation. 1880's. Photo by J. Czechowicz

characters was banned. Polish newspapers, theatre and all Polish schools were closed down. Many Catholic churches were converted to Orthodox ones, both the Polish and Lithuanian languages disappeared from public life. Anti-Semitism and Russification of Jews gained force as well.

Countries and cities continue to develop even under severe occupation: Vilnius was no exception. During the entire 19th century industry was developing, new links with the world were established, and new civilizational patterns took root. In 1837–38 an optic telegraph station was set up on the St. Petersburg–Warsaw line (the tower of the Higher Castle was used for that purpose). In 1836 work of the construction of St. George Avenue (now Gedimino Ave.) – the

central Vilnius street – started, and in 1875 the plan of the Naujamiestis district was mapped out and put into effect. Gas lanterns were erected for lighting the city. Construction of the railroad connecting St. Petersburg and Warsaw was started in 1858, and on September 4th, 1860 the first train arrived in Vilnius. Some time later the railroad connected the city with Koenigsberg, Berlin and Paris. Gas, furniture, textile, cigarette and chocolate factories, breweries and hide workshops started to operate; on the other hand, craftsmen guilds disappeared – the last ones were eliminated in 1893. In 1886 the first telephones were installed. From 1893 to 1915 a horse-pulled tram operated. It connected the railroad terminal, the city centre and Užupis and Antakalnis suburbs. In 1899 the first five kilometres of underground sewage pipes were laid, and in 1905 the first cars appeared. From 1901 a small electric power station produced electric power for the lighting of the city hall (now the Philharmonic Society), and on February 1st 1903 the city electric power station on the right bank of the Neris, in front of the Higher Castle, was put into operation. In that year there were 90 factories in Vilnius, among which Petras Vileišis' metal factory should be mentioned separately; Vileišis used to assign part of its revenue for the needs of Lithuanian culture.

1 Jan Kazimierz Wilczyński (1806–85). 1830. Art. Richerrs
2 Ludwik Kondratowicz-Władysław Syrokomla (1823–62).
From *Album de Wilna* by Jan Kazimierz Wilczyński
3 Eustachy Tyszkiewicz (1814–73). Ca. 1860. Photo by A. Swieykowski
4 Panorama of Vilnius from Saltoniškės. 1860. Art. M.E. Andriolli
5 Stanisław Moniuszko (1819–72). 1850. Art. A. Lafosse
6 Sacristy of the Bernardine Church painted by the graduate
of Ivan Trutnev's art school L. Balzukevičiūtė

Opposite p.: Exhibition of the Museum of Antiquities in the Smuglewicz hall
of Vilnius University in 1857–65. From *Album de Wilna* by Jan Kazimierz Wilczyński

# Culture at the turn of the century

However, the old capital of Lithuania at that time was more similar to a provincial town than a metropolis, with badly paved streets, without advanced utilities, full of provincial low-rank gentry, petty craftsmen, beggars, Russian officials and clerks. After the university and the majority of cultural institutions were closed, there was a lack of intellectuals. True, in 1856 the well-known archaeologist Eustachy Tyszkiewicz founded the Museum of Antiquities, and in 1867 the state public library was opened. Vilnius was home to several

writers, artists and musicians, mainly Poles: poet Ludwik Kondratowicz-Władysław Syrokomla, painter Alfred Roemer, composer Stanisław Moniuszko, whose famous opera *Halka* was produced in Vilnius in 1854 and 1860. Some of them were related with Lithuanian culture as well – in their work they drew on the themes of Lithuanian history and painted portraits of outstanding Lithuanians.

The repressive tsarist politics could not entirely suppress Vilnius cultural life. The cultured society resisted Russification, but several Russian voices joined this dialogue as well. Vilnius experienced the influence of a Russian theatre and particularly an art school founded by Ivan Trutnev: it taught the basics of art to many Lithuanian artists (Juozas Zikaras, Vladas Didžiokas, Rapolas Jakimavičius, Vytautas Kairiūkštis) and Jewish modernists who later won world fame – Chaim Soutine and Jacques Lipschitz. Vilnius was the childhood

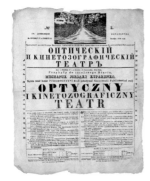

1, 2, 4 Posters of events held in Vilnius in the 19th cent.

3 A Lithuanian woman with *verbos*. 1847. Art. K. Rusiecki

5 Jewish vendors in the environs of Vilnius. From *Album de Wilna* by Jan Kazimierz Wilczyński

Opposite p.: Vilnius fashions in the early 19th cent.

Illustrations for the magazine *Tygodnik Wileński* (1815–22)

city of the famous Russian philosopher Mikhail Bakhtin (1895–1975), whose basic contribution to the world culture is, characteristically, his penetrating analysis of the concept of dialogue.

In the 2nd half of the 19th cent. the Lithuanian national revival movement gained momentum not so much in Vilnius, where the number of Lithuanian-speaking people was relatively small, but west of the city – in Tilžė (Tilsit), Kaunas and Seinai (Sejny). However, Vilnius was regarded by Lithuanians as their historical capital, an indubitable centre of national life and the future national state. The roots of the Polish-Lithuanian conflict lie in this era. Many Poles held an attitude that Vilnius was a purely Polish rather than multi-cultural city; Lithuanians on their turn considered it purely Lithuanian. Both ethnic groups appropriated the tradition of the Grand Duchy of Lithuania as their own. This conflict soon told on the fate of Vilnius. It should be noted that in the

struggle for Vilnius the Poles had certain advantages, if only for the fact that they were a much larger nation that had already built a rich culture. Lithuanian culture developed under extremely difficult conditions – books and newspapers in Latin characters banned by the tsarist government were published abroad and were smuggled into Lithuania and Vilnius. However, in the early 20th cent. Lithuanians managed to establish the press and create literature; their public life developed so intensely that it raised hopes for autonomy and even independence. The Belorussian national movement, for the most part also associated with Vilnius, was weaker and maintained quite close links with the Lithuanian movement.

Throughout the 19th cent. Vilnius remained a major centre of Jewish culture and spiritual life. For example, the famous printing house of the Romm family published the Babylonian Talmud in Vilnius (note that Jewish publishing houses also published books in other languages, including Lithuanian). The majority of Jews were Orthodox, but adherents of Jewish Enlightenment (Haskalah) were also appearing. As long as Vilnius University was operating, Jews were

1 Vilnius Jews. Postcard published during the First World War in Germany
2 Stiklių Street in Vilnius. 1910. Art. Stanisław Fleury  3 Bima of the Great Synagogue. 1937. Photo by J. Bułhak
4 Aron ha kodesh cartouche with two tablets with God's commandments in the Great Synagogue
Opposite p.: Žydų Street before the Second World War. 1937. Photo by J. Bułhak

allowed to study medicine and occasionally also natural sciences; later the Jewish Teachers' Institute, the only one in the Russian empire, was founded. In 1860–80 the Hebrew weekly *Ha-Karmel* was published in Vilnius; in 1892 the famous Strashun library was established; in 1904 a Hebrew daily was launched. The sculptor Mark Antokolski, violinist Jasha Heifetz, many writers who wrote in Hebrew and Yiddish, numerous religious and social figures, doctors, journalists who became famous not only in Lithuania, but also in other countries, descend from Vilnius Jews. It would not be an exaggeration to claim that without Vilnius the state of Israel would not have been founded. The city was the major centre of Zionism in the Russian empire, and enabled the Jews to retain their cultural uniqueness, so important for Israel's national identity, better than

Wilna. Jüdische Straße

anywhere else. In 1897 the Bund – the Yiddish socialist party – was founded in Vilnius. The city became the symbolic capital of this (now almost extinct) language and Yiddish literature. Later a Jewish national theatre company began its activity. It successfully performed the play *Dybbuk* by S. An-ski (Solomon Rapoport) in various countries; even today the repertory of the Israel National Theatre contains this classical play. In politics the Jews usually sided with Lithuanians and Belorussians; all three groups held joint cultural projects – exhibitions and concerts.

Cultural activity in Vilnius gained intensity in the early 20th cent. In 1904 the Lithuanians won their struggle for their own press: the ban to use the Latin alphabet was lifted. In 1905 Vilnius, as well as the whole empire, was shaken by a revolution. On December 4th–5th of the same year, the Great Seimas of Vilnius – the Lithuanian congress – took place in the city; democracy and Lithuania's autonomy were among its demands. The Russian authorities started to yield ground. The banned and suppressed ethnic traditions and movements re-

1 Poster of the post-mortem exhibition by M.K. Čiurlionis. 1911
2 Poster of the 1st exhibition of Lithuanian art in Vilnius. 1907
3 Jonas Basanavičius (1851–1927). 1905. Photo by A. Jurašaitis
4 Mikalojus Konstantinas Čiurlionis (1875–1911). 1908. Photo by S. Fleury
5 Medal commemorating the 20th anniversary of the Great Seimas of Vilnius. 1925. Art. P. Rimša
Opposite p.: Participants of the congress of the Lithuanian Scholarly Society:
(sitting from left to right) J. Jablonskis, J. Žymantienė-Žemaitė, P. Kriaučiūnas, J. Basanavičius,
L. Didžiulienė-Žmona, J. Dielininkaitis; (in the 2nd row) V. Polukaitis, A. Vileišis,
the fourth – A. Sketeris, G. Landsbergis-Žemkalnis, J. Ambrozaitis; (in the 3rd row) J. Kairiūkštis,
J. Spudulis, M. Davainis-Silvestraitis, M. Kuprevičius. 1912. Photo by A. Jurašaitis

emerged. Both Lithuanians and Poles derived benefit from this fact. Their languages were no longer forbidden in public places, schools etc. The cultural movement of both nations in Vilnius developed in parallel directions; it should be said that Lithuanians frequently left the Poles behind. Thus, the first Lithuanian daily *Vilniaus žinios* (Vilnius News) appeared in 1904, while the Polish daily *Kurier Litewski* – in 1905. The Lithuanian Art Society was also established a year earlier (1907) than its Polish equivalent; its leading member was the painter and musician Mikalojus Konstantinas Čiurlionis. From 1905 Lithuanian theatre companies started their activity (on November 6th 1906 the first Lithuanian opera *Birutė* was

produced), while the Polish theatre of Nuna Młodziejowska operated in 1908–10 (later other Polish theatres appeared). Realist and modernist literature in Lithuanian (Žemaitė, Lazdynų Pelėda, Vincas Krėvė, Liudas Gira, Kazys Binkis) and Polish (Czesław Jankowski, Helena Roemer-Ochenkowska, Zdzisław Kleszczyński) developed in Vilnius. The Lithuanian Scholarly Society led by the historian, ethnologist and journalist Jonas Basanavičius, called the patriarch of the Lithuanian nation, was established at the same time as the Polish Society of Lovers of Science (1907). In 1915 in Vilnius, at that time occupied by Germans, the first Lithuanian high school was opened. Thoughts about the restoration of the university were in the air; Lithuanian, Polish and Russian were suggested as the basic languages of teaching.

Before the 1905 revolution, 15 periodical publications, all Russian, were in circulation in Vilnius, while in 1911 their number increased to 69, among them 35 Polish, 20 Lithuanian, 7 Russian, 5 Jewish and 2 Belorussian. Various groups both competed and collaborated. The newly emerging trend of Polish intellectuals *krajowcy* (Michał Roemer and others) tried to maintain the tradition of the

1 Central market of Vilnius (Hala). 1900's
2 Composer Konstantin Galkovski (1875–1963). 1924
3 St. George Avenue. Postcard published during the First World War in Germany
4 The German army on St. George Avenue during the Kaiser's visit in 1915.
Postcard from the series "War in the East"
5 Badge of graduation from the Vilnius Military School. 1915

multi-national Grand Duchy and emphasized the difference between Lithuania and Poland. The Lithuanian culture historian Mykolas Biržiška collaborated with the *krajowcy*. Two Lithuanian periodicals – *Litwa* and *Lud* – were published in Polish and promulgated pro-Lithuanian ideas. A number of Vilnius' men of letters wrote in several languages, several artists – e.g. Antanas Vivulskis (Antoni Wiwulski), who created the monument of Three Crosses – could be regarded both Lithuanian and Polish. The painter Ferdynand Ruszczyc, one of the first admirers of Čiurlionis, dedicated an entire issue of the magazine *Tygodnik Wileński* to Lithuanian art. The Pole Ludomir Michał Rogowski wrote music to the poem "Who Is Coming Out There" by the Belorussian poet Janka Kupala that later became an unofficial Belorussian anthem. Rogowski's colleague, the local Russian Konstantin Galkovski (Galkauskas), created The Lithuanian Rhapsody and a cantata in honour of Basanavičius. Lithuanians actively collaborated with Belorussians – Janka Kupala, Jakub Kolas, Vaclav Lastouski, Alaiza Paškevič (Ciotka), – who published in Vilnius the weekly *Naša Niva* (1906–15). This collaboration in several cases culminated in family ties. *Naša Niva* and Belorussian books were published in Martynas Kukta's Lithuanian printing house and sold in Marija Šlapelienė's Lithuanian bookshop.

Vilnius differs from many Central European and Baltic cities in that it virtually lacks monuments of the Jugend style. In the early 20th, as well as late 19th cent., new houses were mainly built in the Russian garrison style that compared poorly with the Gothic, Renaissance and Baroque buildings. The culture of cafes was also missing, particularly in comparison with such cities of the Austrian-Hungarian Empire as Krakow and Lviv. In 1910 the city had 88 restaurants, 97 dining and tea rooms, 43 hotels and as many as 450 pubs. Famous were Vilnius fairs, particularly the so-called "Kaziukas" on St. Casimir's day (March 4th) – this tradition has survived into our days. In 1906 a roofed market close to the railroad terminal and the Gate of Dawn, the so-called Hala, was opened. In 1915 Vilnius had a population of ca. 180 000 inhabitants.

# The First World War and struggles for Vilnius

This peculiar period in the life of Vilnius ended with the First World War. In the autumn of 1915 the army of the German Kaiser Wilhelm II occupied the city. When Germany started to lose the war, an opportunity of restoring both Lithuania's and Poland's independence presented itself. On September 17th–23rd 1917 Vilnius hosted the Lithuanian conference that elected the Lithuanian Council consisting of 20 public figures; the most famous of them were Jonas Basanavičius and Antanas Smetona.

On February 16th 1918 the Council proclaimed the restoration of the independent Lithuanian state with the capital Vilnius, and broke off Lithuania's former relations with other states.

PIRMOJI LIETUVOS VALSTYBĖS TARYBA,
kuri 1918 m. vasario mėn. 16 d. pasirašė Lietuvos Nepriklausomybės aktą.

Iš kairės į dešinę sėdi: J. Vileišis, dr. J. Šaulys, kun. J. Staugaitis, St. Narutavičius, dr. J. Basanavičius, A. Smetona, kan. K. Šaulys, Stp. Kairys, p. Smilgevičius. Stovi: K. Bizauskas, J. Vailokaitis, Donatas Malinauskas, kun. Vl. Mironas, M. Biržiška, kun. A. Petrulis, S. Banaitis, P. Klimas, A. Stulginskis, J. Šernas, Pr. Dovydaitis.

*Premier Conseil d'Etat Lithuanien qui a signé, le 16 février 1918, l'acte proclamant l'indépendance de la Lithuanie*

JÓZEF PIŁSUDSKI
PIERWSZY MARSZAŁEK POLSKI

1 Members of the Lithuanian Council, signatories of the Independence Act.
From: *Album in Commemoration of Vytautas the Great's 500th Anniversary of Death.* Kaunas, 1933
2 At a Vilnius market. Late 19th–early 20th cent. Photo by S. Fleury
3 Józef Piłsudski (1867–1935). 1920's–30's
4 Symbolic keys of Vilnius presented to commandant Józef Piłsudski in 1919. Photo by J. Bułhak

The new state found itself in a very difficult situation. Vilnius was still occupied by the German army, and Germany hoped to make Lithuania its satellite. In Russia the Bolshevik revolution had just taken place: Lenin, Trotsky and Stalin's government was attempting to introduce their regime in Lithuania with the help of local communists led by Vincas Mickevičius-Kapsukas. Finally, the restored Poland led by Józef Piłsudski wanted to form a union or confederation with Lithuania and regarded Vilnius as a Polish city.

Vilnius changed hands many times. It was occupied first by Bolsheviks, then by Poles. The Lithuanian government, having moved to Kaunas, demanded the return of the capital to Lithuania and recognition of the country in its ethnographic lands embracing, in the opinion of Lithuanians, not only Vilnius, but sizeable areas east and south of the city. At the beginning of 1919 a war between Poland and Soviet Russia broke out, and on July 14th 1920 Vilnius was again invaded by Bolsheviks who on August 27th transferred it to Lithuania. The Lithuanian government ruled the city for a month and a half. In early October Józef Piłsudski assigned to General Lucjan Żeligowski the task of capturing Vilnius. Since the international law was on Lithuania's side, Piłsudski and Żeligowski staged a rebellion: Polish units, having supposedly refused to obey the Warsaw government, on October 9th forced the Lithuanians out of Vilnius and established in the city and its environs a bizarre state – the so-called "Middle Lithuania" (*Litwa Środkowa*). Żeligowski's army was intruding further into Lithuania, towards Kaunas and Šiauliai, but the Lithuanians stopped it about 50 km north of Vilnius, near Širvintos and Giedraičiai. Elections to the Vilnius Sejm were held at the beginning of 1922; however, they were boycotted by Lithuanians, Belorussians and Jews. On February 20th 1922 this exclusively Polish Sejm passed a decision to annex "Middle Lithuania" to Poland. Since that time Vilnius became a district centre, a peripheral borderland city in between independent Lithuania and USSR, which survived on memories of the glorious old times rather than the spirit of modern civilization. Lithuania did not recognize the occupation of Vilnius; according to the Constitution, Vilnius continued to be the capital, while Kaunas acquired an unusual status of a "temporary capital". Lithuanian-Polish relations were severed.

In independent Lithuania Vilnius was considered a city occupied by a foreign power: the Union for the Liberation of Vilnius was established, and the mood of society at large was expressed in the famous poem by Petras Vaičiūnas "Hear, World, we will not rest without Vilnius!" Conversely, the Polish official rhetoric stressed the relation of Vilnius with the restored Polish state. The past of Vilnius and particularly the period of Romanticism were explained as a prelude to this restoration. The fact that Piłsudski descended from the Vilnius region and knew the works by Polish Romantic poets by heart also played a certain role. However, this triumphant rhetoric was increasingly interrupted by notes of doubt and criticism, and later a premonition of an approaching catastrophe.

1 Vilnius Bishop Jurgis Matulaitis-Matulevičius (1871–1925). 1922
2 Flood in Vilnius in April 1931. Photo by B. Brudner
3 Tadeusz Wróblewski (1858–1925). "A. Strauss" studio
4 At Rudnicki's café. 1934   5, 6 Jubilee medal of Vilnius University. 1929

# The inter-war period

During this period the cultural life of the city developed mainly in the Polish language. On October 11th 1919 Vilnius (Wilno) University was reopened and named in honour of Stephen Batory. An Art Academy and Conservatoire were established, and in 1930 the Institute of Eastern European Studies was founded. In 1925 the lawyer Tadeusz Wróblewski donated to the city an excellent library (now this library belongs to the Lithuanian Academy of the Sciences). There were several theatre companies – "Reduta", "Lutnia", and others; a lot of art exhibitions were held, literary events used to take place in the so-called Conrad cell, where Mickiewicz with his friends was once imprisoned. Several outstanding Polish writers – Witold Hulewicz, Jerzy Jankowski, Konstanty Ildefons Gałczyński, Stanisław and Józef Mackiewicz – worked in Vilnius; in time a literary group "Żagary" emerged, whose central figure was Czesław Miłosz, a Nobel prize winner-to-be. Literary celebrities from other countries used to visit the city as well, among them Dmitry Merezhkovsky and Gilbert Keith Chesterton. Intellectuals of Vilnius frequented cafes (Rudnicki's, Sztral's) and cabarets.

In 1937 114 newspapers and magazines were published in Vilnius, among them 74 Polish, 16 Jewish, 12 Belorussian, 9 Lithuanian and 3 Russian. However, all ethnic groups except the Poles were increasingly isolated and ousted to the fringes of society. At first the Lithuanians still maintained some influence in city life (in 1918–25 Vilnius Bishop was the Lithuanian Jurgis Matulaitis, later pronounced the Blessed One). But soon the authorities started to persecute Lithuanians, closed down their schools and cultural institutions, arrested them and banished Lithuanian public figures to Kaunas. Belorussians found themselves in a similar position. Though Lithuanian and Belorussian scientific societies, high schools and the Lithuanian theatre "Vaidila" continued to operate, their activity was increasingly limited (on January 1st 1938 the Polish authorities sealed up all property of the Lithuanian Scholarly Society).

In 1925 a unique cultural centre – the YIVO scholarly institute – was established in Vilnius; it focused on the studies of the Yiddish language, local Jewish folklore and traditions, and boasted a large library – 40,000 volumes and many valuable manuscripts. Members of the honorary presidium of the Institute were Sigmund Freud and Albert Einstein. However, YIVO had to endure isolation and increasing anti-Semitism.

Certain facts of cultural interaction among different groups in this period are worth mentioning. The tradition of the Vilnius dialogue was maintained by *krajowcy*, to whom, incidentally, Tadeusz Wróblewski also belonged. The Polish elite that held broad views and understood that the former territory of the Grand Duchy was multi-cultural, assembled at the Institute of Eastern European Studies. The "Żagary" group maintained a very critical attitude to Polish nationalism – it was not by accident that it chose a Lithuanian word for

1 Polish theatre "Lutnia". 1924. Photo by Jan Bułhak
2 Guard of the Lithuanian army on the Hill of Three Crosses
3 Czesław Miłosz. 1935  4 Title page of the 1st issue of *Żagary*. 1931
5 Logo of YIVO  6 Logo of the "Jung Vilne" group. Art. B. Michtom
Opposite p.: Board of the drama section of the Union of Lithuanian Students in Vilnius:
(from the left) Barbora Gaidelytė, Aleksandras Stasiūnas,
Juozapas Kanopka (chairman of the section), Pranas Žemaitis, Aldona Liobytė

its name ("žagarai" means "twigs"); Czesław Miłosz, who calls himself "the last citizen of the Grand Duchy of Lithuania", gradually became a similar symbol of the Lithuanian and Polish cultural bond as Adam Mickiewicz was in the 19th cent. Young Vilnius Lithuanian poets Juozas Kėkštas and Albinas Žukauskas, as well as certain Belorussians, experienced the influence of the "Žagary" group. In the Jewish literary milieu an approximate equivalent to the "Žagary" was the group "Jung Vilne" (Abraham Sutzkever, Chaim Grade and others). Lithuanian artists Vytautas Kairiūkštis and Vladas Drėma joined not only the Lithuanian, but also Polish modernist movement.

The premonitions of catastrophe current among Vilnius intellectuals, particularly manifested in the activities of the "Žagary" group, started to come true at the close of the thirties. On August 23rd 1939, Hitler's Germany and Stalin's

USSR divided Europe into zones of influence and signed the secret Molotov-Ribbentrop pact. This untied Hitler's hands: on September 1st he attacked Poland, starting the Second World War. Germany encouraged Lithuania to join the attack and take Vilnius back, but Lithuania proclaimed neutrality and provided help to interned Polish soldiers. The USSR intruded into the territories ruled by Poland from the east, on September 19th occupied Vilnius, and on October 10th by a special decree ceded it to Lithuania. On October 26th the Lithuanian army marched into the plundered capital. However, the rule of independent Lithuania lasted briefly: in June–July 1940 the USSR forcefully occupied the entire country including Vilnius.

During its short rule the Lithuanian government restructured Stephen Batory's University into a Lithuanian one. This, as well as other attempts at rapid Lithuanization of Vilnius, created substantial friction between Lithuanians and Poles, though the situation of the Poles in Vilnius was incomparably better than in areas occupied by the Nazis or Soviets. The Polish government in exile continued to regard Vilnius as belonging to Poland. The quarrel about Vilnius lasted at least until 1945 and cost some bloodshed for both nations, though for the most part it was overshadowed by disasters brought by new occupations.

1 Parade of the October Revolution on November 7th 1940

2 Poster of the Vilnius ghetto announcing a ceremonial meeting on the occasion of the 100,000th book checked out of the ghetto library on December 13th 1942

3 The Great Synagogue after the Second World War. 1944. Photo by S. Urbanavičiūtė-Subačiuvienė

4 German captives on Vilnius streets on July 15th 1944

Opposite p.: Parade of the German army in 1941

# The Second World War and post-war occupation

The Soviet rule in 1940–41 brought grave consequences for Vilnius. Many Vilnius residents – Lithuanians, Poles and Jews – were deported to Siberia, particularly at the beginning of June 1941. Numerous people were executed. Therefore, when Germany attacked USSR on June 22nd 1941, more than one inhabitant of Vilnius greeted the German army as a liberating force. Yet hopes of restoring independent Lithuania were doomed to dissipate soon. The Nazis occupied Vilnius already on the third day of the war and immediately introduced a harsh occupational regime; it brought much suffering for the entire city

population, but firstly for the Jews whom the Hitlerites condemned to death. Approx. 42,000 Jews were driven to a ghetto. The majority of them were killed in Aukštieji Paneriai, where the Nazis and their Lithuanian and other local collaborators conducted mass executions. The war destroyed nearly the entire large community of Vilnius Jews.

Lithuanian, Polish and Jewish resistance movements were active in Vilnius; unfortunately, they did not maintain any significant communication. The Lithuanian Vilnius University that had turned into a centre of resistance, was closed down by the occupiers on March 17th 1943, and 60 Lithuanian intellectuals were sent to the Stuthoff concentration camp. Later the University went underground (that was also the fate of Polish Stephen Batory's University). Many Lithuanians and Poles, particularly the clergy, were helping Jews. Lithuanians, Poles, Belorussians and even Jews in the ghetto tried to maintain at least minimal cultural life in their communities. These activities were conducted in the shadow of death.

On July 13th 1944 Vilnius was again occupied by the Soviet army. Units of the Polish guerrilla army – Armia Krajowa – also marched into Vilnius, but the

1 First secretary of the Lithuanian Communist Party Antanas Sniečkus (1903–74)
at voluntary work at the construction of the Sports Palace in Vilnius
2 Bishop Vincentas Borisevičius (b. 1887), shot in Vilnius in 1946
3 The first song festival in Vilnius. July 21st 1946
4 Concert commemorating the 33rd anniversary of the liberation of Vilnius
from the Nazis in Vingio Park. 1977
Opposite p.: Meeting on the occasion of unveiling the monument to V. Mickevičius-Kapsukas.
05 11 1962. At the microphone – A. Sniečkus

Soviets immediately disarmed them and arrested most of the Polish fighters. A new occupation began – this time it lasted for almost five decades.

The period of Soviet occupation, like the one of tsarist Russia's occupation, was far from homogeneous. The most tragic period were the years 1944–53 (until Stalin's death). In these years the Lithuanian resistance movement was suppressed, many citizens were killed and deported, and total ideological control was imposed. After 1953 and particularly after 1956 the Soviet regime somewhat softened; however, it remained as totalitarian and oppressive as before. During that time passive resistance dominated, slowly acquiring the features of independent cultural trends, underground activity, and even legalistic opposition.

Military actions destroyed ca. 40 percent of Vilnius buildings, but luckily, almost all architectural monuments survived. Only the ghetto area with the famous Great Synagogue, whose walls were pulled down after the war by the Communist authorities, was totally destroyed. Still, the Soviets closed down the majority of churches and blew up some famous structures of the city – the Calvary chapels and the monument of Three Crosses. To a certain degree, the city was corrupted by buildings characteristic of the socialist realism style. Fortunately, the silhouette of Vilnius and its many-layered architectural halo was retained: that is why Vilnius was more suitable for dignified life than typical Soviet cities. The composition of the population changed radically. In 1945–46 and later more than 100,000 Poles left for Poland (including a small number of Lithuanians who were trying to avoid Soviet repressions). New arrivals were Lithuanians from Kaunas and other Lithuanian cities and towns, Belorussians from neighbouring Belorussian regions, and Russian officials, military and KGB officers, factory workers, mostly from Moscow and elsewhere. Initially the Lithuanian population was not large, but gradually they came to constitute the major part of Vilnius residents.

1 From the left: philosopher Justinas Mikutis (1922–88),
artists Algimantas Stankevičius (b. 1933) and Vincas Kisarauskas (1934–88)

2 Concert of the trio of Viacheslav Ganelin, Vladimir Tarasov and Vladimir Chekasin
at the Philharmonic Society. 1970's. Photo by G. Talas

3 Armed Soviet soldiers against the participants of the meeting
held by the Lithuanian Freedom League to denounce the 2nd secret protocol
of the Molotov-Ribbentrop pact. 28 09 1988. Photo by V. Kliukas

Opposite p.: Exhibition of works by folk artists dedicated to the 60th anniversary of the USSR
on Pilies Lane (present Bernardinų St.)

In the context of the USSR Vilnius was a special city. Through Vilnius the influences of modern Western thought and art, moods and fashions found their way into the Soviet empire. Vilnius boasted the best jazz to be found in the USSR (Viacheslav Ganelin's trio), an original school of painting and graphic art akin to surrealism and expressionism (Jonas Švažas, Vincas Kisarauskas, Petras Repšys), and non-standard films. At the end of the Soviet era a movement of theatrical avant-garde with the world-class director Eimuntas Nekrošius developed. Works by James Joyce and Jorge Luis Borges, banned in Moscow and many Soviet republics, were translated into Lithuanian. Young philosophers of Vilnius University (the school of Eugenijus Meškauskas) did not recognize the

absolute authority of Marxist dogmas. A nonconformist community of artists that Vilnius had not had since 1930's, became a strong factor in the city life.

All these cultural trends were at some level associated with the national and religious resistance. In Lithuania and Vilnius the underground was operating (noteworthy is the unofficial publication *The Chronicle of the Lithuanian Catholic Church*), and in 1970's associations publicly fighting for human rights, such as the Lithuanian Helsinki group (1976), appeared. The atmosphere of openness and relative freedom to be found in Vilnius was quite important for visitors from Moscow and Leningrad (St. Petersburg), including the Nobel prize winner-to-be Joseph Brodsky who devoted a cycle of poems to Lithuania and its capital. Like in the tsarist times, Vilnius was the "third city of the empire", a counterbalance and opposition to its two bureaucratic capitals. It continued to provide a meeting ground for cultural figures of different ethnic groups (side by side with Lithuanians, Russian theatre directors Kama Ginkas and Roman Viktiuk, the Polish poet Alicja Rybałko, the Jewish prose writers Icchok Meras and Grigory Kanovich grew up in Vilnius).

1 Assault of the Television Tower. 13 01 1991. Photo by Z. Nekrošius
2 Dismantling of the monument to Lenin. 22 08 1991. Photo by Z. Nekrošius
Opposite p.: Protest meeting of the "Sajūdis" on the occasion of the 49th anniversary
of Molotov-Ribbentrop pact in Vingio park. 23 08 1988. Photo by R. Urbakavičius

# Liberation

From 1987 on, as the Soviet empire began to disintegrate, demonstrations against the regime took place in Vilnius – they started at the monument to Adam Mickiewicz. In 1988 a newly established informal public organization "Sajūdis" took on the fight for independence. On March 11th 1990 the Supreme Council of Lithuania (the future Seimas) proclaimed the act "On the restoration of the independent state of Lithuania". Moscow's authorities, attempting to halt the crumbling of the empire, attacked the Vilnius Television Tower on January 13th 1991. Fourteen independence fighters were killed by bullets and tanks. The building of the Parliament (Seimas) was in serious danger – it was surrounded by barricades, but the occupiers did not dare to attack members of

the parliament and a large crowd defending them. It was a signal for the final fall of the USSR. In August 1991 the reborn Lithuanian state was internationally recognized. Russia, Poland and Belorussia, having signed agreements with Lithuania, by the same token renounced their claims to Lithuania's capital.

One of the embodiments of the Vilnius myth is the city's emblem (banned in the Soviet times), representing St. Christopher carrying the Infant Christ across the river. The emblem is considered by some to reach back to pagan times and to represent a legendary Lithuanian hero carrying his wife across the waters. However it may be interpreted, one can perceive the Vilnius emblem as a baroque allegory: the constantly changing generations are carrying Lithuania's capital and its many-faceted culture through the river of history, its disasters and dangers, to the future.

# Monuments of History and Culture

oethe once stated: the further one swims into the sea, the deeper it gets – the same can be said about Rome. These words can also be applied to Vilnius, called by travellers "the little Rome" and similar names. One can make a superficial acquaintance of the Lithuanian capital in two or three days, but an in-depth study of its historical and cultural heritage could take twenty or thirty years, probably an entire lifetime. The many-layered Vilnius, whose monuments range from pagan times up to the 20th century, offers much to be explored. New, often sensational data about already familiar places keep coming to the surface, new art and culture monuments, unknown to former historians, are being discovered. Many recent discoveries have come as a surprise to the author of this guide as well.

Seal of Vilnius, in force probably from 14th cent.

This guide presents brief factual data about Vilnius squares, streets and lanes, churches and palaces, ordinary buildings, courtyards and nooks. They are intended to help the reader orient himself or herself in the labyrinth of the city. The unique and diverse old town of Vilnius is one of the largest in Central and Eastern Europe; even the newer parts of the city have inherited its irregular, organic planning principle. However, while roaming around the old and new city, one should not rely solely on books. One should walk without haste and let oneself get carried away by accident and whim, be attentive to details and fragments, and always look for new, yet unnoticed vantage points. Southern architecture beneath the northern sky, the Vilnius amphitheatre nestled among steep hills, invaded by groves and barren areas, summer cumuli and autumn haze – all this forms a surprisingly uniform, though unplanned, ensemble. It radiates the spirit of freedom and individuality typical of Europe.

## Vilnius castles and the Cathedral

The heart of the city is at the confluence of the Neris and Vilnia rivers. It is also the heart of all Lithuania, the place where the early Lithuanian state was built and grand dukes lived. Since olden times it was the country's religious centre as well – first a place of pagan rituals, and from Lithuania's Christianization till our days – the major centre of Christianity, symbolized by St. Casimir's Chapel in the Cathedral holding the remains of Lithuania's patron saint.

The two rivers, at the confluence of which Gediminas founded his capital, are very different: the Neris, also called the Vilija, is not wide, though quite swift, while the Vilnia that has forced its course among high and steep hills reminds us of a mountain stream. Nearby rises the Gediminas hill with steep 48 m high slopes; on its top looms the Higher, or Gediminas Castle, a symbol of Vilnius

Buildings of the Higher and Lower Castle

and Lithuania. Once the Vilnia had a different riverbed, south and west of the hill, around the present Cathedral Square. Its second riverbed east of the hill was dug out in the late 13th cent. or early 14th cent. In the long run the old riverbed disappeared and only the new one remained, but in the times of Gediminas and his descendants the castle and the Cathedral were situated on a kind of island. On the other bank of the Vilnia rise several hills bearing the names of Three Crosses, Bekesh, Table and Gediminas' Grave. Their steep, thickly overgrown slopes divided by gullies lend the centre of Vilnius an ambience of a foothill city. In early times there was a timber fortification called the Crooked Castle and surrounding settlements on the other side of the Vilnia.

At the foot of the Gediminas Hill stretches the Šventaragis valley, where, according to a legend, remains of the deceased grand dukes used to be burned in pagan times. Westwards of the hill are the excavated remains of the Lower Castle. Somewhat further, on a granite-paved square, stands the Cathedral Basilica, the most remarkable Classical monument in Vilnius, which has preserved traces of many earlier epochs. The belfry of the Cathedral is built on a defensive tower of the Lower Castle.

Remains of the building
of the Higher Castle

## The Higher Castle and the Hill Park ① ②

The Gediminas Hill is a typical Lithuanian mound, the largest such hill of natural origin in Lithuania. The Vilnius castle was first mentioned on October 2nd 1323 in Gediminas' treaty with the city and bishop of Riga and the German order. At that time the Higher Castle was built of timber. Later (the exact date is not known) a brick castle was built. Teutonic knights aided by English, French, Italian and Flemish knights attacked the castle eight times, but not a single attack succeeded. After the 1419 fire Vytautas rebuilt and fortified it. The castle was surrounded by a stone wall, ca. 320 m long, with three towers; in the courtyard stood a three-storey Gothic palace of the grand duke, St. Martin's Chapel and other buildings. In 1610 a noblemen's prison was set up there. The castle was badly damaged in 1655–61, during a war with the Moscow tsar Aleksei Mikhailovich, and was not rebuilt later. During the 1831 uprising, by the tsar's order the Gediminas Hill was turned into part of the Vilnius stronghold – it was encircled by ramparts with bastions and a moat. Of the castle towers, only the western one remained without its upper storeys – in 1837–38 in their place a wooden superstructure for the optical cable was built, later to be converted into a café. In 1930 the superstructure was pulled down, and the third brick storey was reconstructed. The tower was damaged once more during the Second World War, and renovated in 1956–60 to hold a museum. On the tower various occupational powers used to raise their flags. Since 1988 the Lithuanian tricolour is flying there again.

Western tower
of the Higher Castle

The western tower of the Higher Castle, usually called the Gediminas Tower, has an octagonal plan, stone foundation, and mainly brick walls built in the Gothic manner. It is the main survey site of Vilnius offering an excellent view of the old town with its church spires, the city centre and the Neris and Vilnia valleys – the entire amphitheatre of Vilnius terracing down from woody hills to the confluence. Newer housing developments can be seen on the right bank of the Neris.

At the Gediminas Tower loom the remnants of the defensive wall – ca. 10 m on the south side and ca. 22 m on the north side. There are more remnants on the hilltop. The bottom segments of the square southern tower and the northern gate have also survived.

Remnants of the Gothic residential palace occupy the eastern part of the castle territory. The palace had pointed Gothic arches and vaults, its walls were ca. 4 m thick. They are interesting not so much from the viewpoint of their architecture, but as a unique historic legacy bearing witness to the earliest epoch of the Lithuanian capital. The first floor with four rooms has survived in quite a good shape. On the second floor there was a large hall with columns. The palace was partly reconstructed in the recent years.

Three Crosses

The castle tower offers a good view of the Three Crosses – a white monument on the other side of the Vilnia, on a hill, also called the Hill of Three Crosses (or the Barren Hill). This structure has become one of the symbols of Vilnius. Like Christ's statue crowning Rio de Janeiro, it completes the silhouette of the city. The history of the Three Crosses goes back to the times of Algirdas. According to a legend, pagans killed seven Franciscan missionaries in Vilnius. The monks were buried on the hill. In memory of these monks a chapel was erected, and in the 17th cent. three wooden crosses depicted in early drawings of the city were built. In 1869 they collapsed, and the tsarist authorities forbade their restoration. In 1916 architect Antanas Vivulskis (Antoni Wiwulski) built concrete crosses. In 1951 the Soviet authorities blew them up, but in 1989, before the proclamation of independence, they were re-erected. Today the crosses are taller (by 1.8 m) than those designed by Vivulskis. Fragments of the old crosses are displayed nearby.

Farther away looms the Bekesh Hill with steep slopes named after the Hungarian Caspar Bekesh (1520–79), a military leader in the service of Stephen Batory, who was buried there: as an Arian he could not rest in a Catholic cemetery. On Bekesh's grave an octagonal monument with an inscription was erected, but in 1843 it collapsed, the Vilnia having washed away the slope. A concrete pavilion, now a landmark of the Bekesh Hill, has nothing in common with this monument. The Hill of Gediminas' Grave, most probably a mound, can be seen behind the Bekesh Hill. According to one tradition, Gediminas was buried there, though another tradition points to Veliuona, where he was killed, as his burial place. It is worthwhile climbing the Hills of Three Crosses and Bekesh. A view opening from these hills is no less beautiful than the one from the Gediminas Tower, and perhaps even better, as it allows one to see the Castle Tower itself.

The Crooked Castle apparently stood on the Hill of Three Crosses. There, as well as on the Bekesh Hill, archaeologists have discovered remains of burnt homesteads and 13th and 14th cent. finds.

## The Lower Castle ③

The palace at the foot of the Castle Hill was a residence of the Grand Duke. In the 2nd half of the 14th cent. the palace and other buildings of the Lower Castle were surrounded by a defensive wall with four gates, more than 1 km long: the present Pilies Street started at the first gate, Tilto Street – at the second gate, the third gate was situated at the present Pilies (Castle) Bridge and the beginning

Plan of Vilnius castles
1. Castle Gate
2. Monument to Gediminas
3. Cathedral Square
4. Bishops' Palace
5. Belfry
6. Cathedral

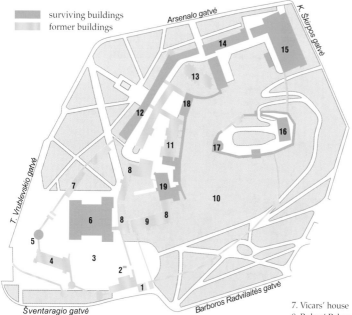

surviving buildings
former buildings

7. Vicars' house
8. Rulers' Palace of the Lower Castle
9. Archaeology exhibition of the Rulers' Palace
10. Park of the Rulers' Palace
11. Office premises
12. New Arsenal (National Museum)
13. Foundations of the Church of St. Anne and St. Barbara
14. Old Arsenal (Archaeology exhibition of the National Museum)
15. Old Arsenal (Museum of Applied Art)
16. Rulers' Palace of the Higher Castle
17. Western Tower of the Higher Castle (Museum)
18. House of the Castle Keeper
19. The east wing of the Rulers' Palace, after 19th cent. reconstruction – A. Šliozbergas' house

of Kosciuškos Street, and the fourth one was on the south side. There were four towers, the Cathedral belfry was later built on the remnants of one of them. In the 15th cent. there were several Gothic buildings in this area besides the palace: the bishop's residence, the arsenal, the tribunal and the vicars' house.

In historical reminiscences the Higher Castle is primarily related with the era of Gediminas, Algirdas and Vytautas, and the Lower Castle – with the times of Sigismund the Old and Sigismund August, Queen Bona and Barbora Radvilaitė. In the 16th cent. it was an Italian-style palace with four wings and attics. They encircled the inner courtyard of 2,500 square metres and were connected to the eastern wall of the Cathedral by a roofed gallery, through which Grand Dukes would go to the Mass. The palace was built by Italian architects Bartolomeo Berecci, Bernardo Zanobi da Gianotis, Giovanni Cini and Vilnius masters. On the southeast there was a park. Quite close to the Neris (in the place of the present library of the Academy of the Sciences) the Radziwiłł estate was located. After the Lublin Union the castle was doomed to deterioration: on

House of the Castle
Keeper

their visits to Vilnius kings would stay in other residencies. The castle was also damaged during the 1655–61 war with Moscow, and in
the early 19th cent. it was pulled down. Today the territory of the
Lower Castle has become a site of archaeological excavations, and
reconstruction plans are under way.

Old Arsenal
(the east wing)

At the Lower Castle a 15th–16th cent. house of the castle keeper
and the 16th cent. foundations of the Church of St. Anne and St.
Barbara have survived. In the late 18th cent. in the eastern part of
the castle, at the Gediminas Hill, prof. Stanislovas Bonifacas
Jundzilas (Stanisław Bonifacy Jundziłł) laid out the university
botanical garden, whose plant collection was one of the most
famous in Europe; however, with the closing of the university, the
garden dwindled to several isolated trees that can hardly be traced
nowadays.

## The Old Arsenal ④

The Old Arsenal (Arsenalo St. 3, 3a) is situated at the Vilnia, at the
foot of the Castle Hill, in the former territory of the Lower Castle.
It is known since the middle of the 16th cent. as a place for storing
weapons produced in a weapon foundry in the area of the present
Tilto St. A Renaissance attic decorated with double-arched niches

New Arsenal

was built in the late 16th – early 17th cent. The building was damaged during civil wars of the 17th cent. and a war with Moscow, rebuilt in 1780, and burned down at the end of the Second World War. In 1986 the east wing was restored according to a project by architect Evaldas Purlys, the exterior was reconstructed on the

basis of iconographic material. Since 1987 it houses the Museum of Applied Art. The interior and exterior of the Old Arsenal enables the visitors to feel the ambience of the Renaissance Vilnius.

Old Arsenal
(the north wing)

## The New Arsenal ⑤

In the 14th cent., buildings adjoining the defensive wall of the Lower Palace stood on the site of the New Arsenal (Arsenalo St. 1). Later, apparently in the 2nd half of the 18th cent., they were connected. Vilnius voivode Michał Kazimierz Ogiński built a palace on the remains of the former building. Architect Martin Knackfuss rendered some Classical features to the New Arsenal. The building has retained fragments of its early Gothic vaults and Renaissance brick walls. In the 19th cent. the New Arsenal housed soldiers' barracks. In 1958–65 the building was renovated and converted into a museum. At the present time it holds a permanent exhibition of history and ethnography of the National Museum of Lithuania.

# Cathedral (Basilica) ⑥

The left (north) nave

It is assumed that in pagan times an altar, a sacred fire or even a Perkūnas sanctuary was located on the site of the present Cathedral of St. Stanislaus and St. Vladislaus in the Šventaragis valley. After being baptized in 1251, Grand Duke Mindaugas probably built the first cathedral on this site. It was a brick building with a massive square tower on the west side. Its remains – foundations and glazed tile floor – were discovered in 1973–76 in the vaults of the present Cathedral. The building contained elements of a transitional style from Romanesque into Gothic: coloured tiles, some of them with ornamental patterns and representing various scenes, are among the earliest monuments of Lithuanian art. After Mindaugas' death (1263) the Cathedral might have been turned into a pagan sanctuary again. The remains of two brick stairs traversing the nave, discovered in 1984 under the floor of the north nave, may have survived from this period. Still, historians do not

The west façade

Statue of a Lithuanian
duke on the south
façade

fully agree about the pre-Christian evolution of the building. In the words of the Polish historian Jan Długosz, at the time of Lithuania's new Christianization (1387) King Jogaila "ordered that the so-called eternal fire kept in Vilnius, the most important city and capital of Lithuania, and kindled with fire-wood by a pagan priest [...] with pagans participating, be extinguished, and the temple with an altar, on which sacrifices were made, be pulled down." On the site of the temple he built a new Gothic cathedral, whose remains have also been discovered in the vaults of the present one. After the 1419 fire Vytautas had the cathedral rebuilt as a magnificent Gothic temple. According to a testimony of the traveller Ghillebert de Lannoy, it was reminiscent of the cathedral in Frombork (Frauenburg) in Prussia and on its façade had twin towers of different height.

Grand Dukes of Lithuania, from Vytautas to the nine-year-old Sigismund August, used to be ceremoniously crowned in the Cathedral. Many of them, as well as a number of outstanding Lithuanian noblemen and bishops, were buried there, though their tombs cannot be easily traced today.

The Cathedral burned several times and was reconstructed and renovated. It acquired certain features of Renaissance, and later – Baroque. Construction works were mainly supervised by Italian architects Annus, Bernardo Zanobi da Gianotis, Giovanni Cini and Constantino Tencalla. In 1623–36 on the initiative of King Sigismund Vasa, the most beautiful part – the Baroque St. Casimir's Chapel – was erected. In September 1769, the south tower of the façade was destroyed by a storm, which caused severe damage to the Cathedral; a priest and six ordinands were killed under the

Bishop Ignacy Massalski. Late 18th cent. Art. Franciszek Smuglewicz

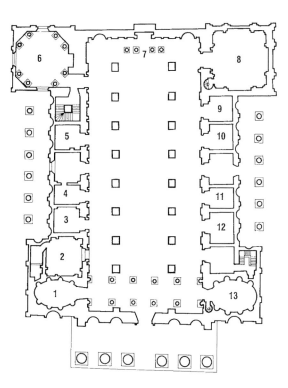

Plan of the Cathedral
1. St. Ladislas' Chapel
2. Wołłowicz (Royal) Chapel
3. Kęsgailos Chapel
4. Chapel of the Saviour's Coffin
5. St. Peter's Chapel
6. Sacristy
7. High altar
8. St. Casimir's Chapel
9. Bishops' Chapel
10. St. Ignatius Loyola's Chapel
11. Montvydai (St. Paul) Chapel
12. Gasztold Chapel
13. Chapel of the Name of the Holy Virgin Mary (Deportees)

ruins. Vilnius Bishop Ignacy Massalski commissioned the best Vilnius architect Laurynas Stuoka-Gucevičius to reconstruct the Cathedral.

Having retained the former Gothic plan of naves and walls, Stuoka-Gucevičius included into it St. Casimir's Chapel and the Royal Wołłowicz Chapel on the opposite corner. The church acquired a strictly geometrical square form typical of French Classicism. In pursuit of symmetry, the architect designed a sacristy in front of St. Casimir's Chapel and crowned it with a cupola. On the west side he built a large portal of six Doric columns with a triangular pediment. The Cathedral became the most monumental purely Classical building in the entire territory of the Commonwealth. After Stuoka-Gucevičius' death it was completed by Michael

Central (great) nave from the high altar side

Schulz: the work was finished in 1820. On the roof above the pediment three sculptures of St. Stanislaus, St. Helen and St. Casimir (sculptor Kazimierz Jelski) were erected. In the times of Soviet occupation the original sculptures were pulled down, to be reconstructed by sculptor Stanislovas Kuzma in 1997.

In 1931, the Neris flooded the Cathedral, and cracks appeared in its walls and vaults. In the process of repairing and conserving several crypts have been discovered, among them crypts with the remains of Alexander Jagiellon and two wives of Sigismund August, Elisabeth and Barbora Radvilaitė (Barbara Radziwiłł). A mausoleum was set up to hold these remains.

The Soviet authorities closed the Cathedral in 1950. From 1956 on, the building housed a picture gallery, concerts of organ music used

Organ face

to be held there. It was not until 1989 that the Cathedral was returned to the Catholics and became the major sanctuary again.

Simple colonnades on the side façades reiterate the monumental columns of the portal. Above St. Casimir's Chapel and the sacristy rise symmetrical brass-plated cupolas. The front and side façades are decorated with sculptures. It seems to be the last trace of Vilnius Baroque in the strict 18th cent. architecture imparting reminiscences of ancient Greece and Rome. The most beautiful sculptures are placed in niches behind the columns of the central portal: Abraham, Moses and the four evangelists with symbolic figures of an angel, a lion, an ox and an eagle. Above them are five high relief compositions on the motifs from the New Testament: the first represents the descent of the Holy Spirit, followed by three miracles of St. Peter and a scene from the life of St. Paul. The tympanum of the pediment represents Noah's sacrifice in an impetuous Baroque style. All these picturesque sculptures and relief works noted for the interplay of light and shadows were created by the Italian artist Tommaso Righi in 1785–91.

Memorial plaque to the grand duke of Lithuania Vytautas

The side façades hold decorative rococo sculptures from the middle of the 18th cent. representing seven Grand Dukes on the south one and five Jesuit saints on the north one. In 1832 they were transferred here from the Church of St. Casimir, which was closed after the 1830–31 uprising.

Attention should be drawn to a memorial plaque commemorating the founding of St. Casimir's Chapel attached to its outer wall. It is a typical Baroque monument from marble and sandstone, apparently created by Constantino Tencalla in 1636. The plaque is decorated with the coat of arms of the Commonwealth – the Polish Eagle and the Lithuanian Vytis (The Knight).

The interior of the Cathedral is also Classical and strict. Four Doric columns of the high altar seem to echo the main façade. In contrast,

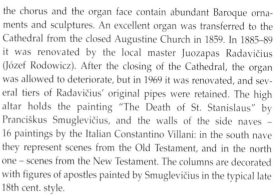

the chorus and the organ face contain abundant Baroque ornaments and sculptures. An excellent organ was transferred to the
Cathedral from the closed Augustine Church in 1859. In 1885–89
it was renovated by the local master Juozapas Radavičius
(Józef Rodowicz). After the closing of the Cathedral, the organ
was allowed to deteriorate, but in 1969 it was renovated, and several tiers of Radavičius' original pipes were retained. The high
altar holds the painting "The Death of St. Stanislaus" by
Pranciškus Smuglevičius, and the walls of the side naves –
16 paintings by the Italian Constantino Villani: in the south nave
they represent scenes from the Old Testament, and in the north
one – scenes from the New Testament. The columns are decorated
with figures of apostles painted by Smuglevičius in the typical late
18th cent. style.

The ends of the side naves, on both sides of the high altar, hold two
statues by Righi: "Love of Your Neighbour" (on the south side) and
"Love of God" (on the north side). There are many epitaphs and
memorial plaques set up in the 17th–20th cent. The most interesting of them seems to be the memorial plaque to Vytautas the Great
in the north nave at the eastern wall. It is made of black marble
with a sandstone frame (sculptor Józef Kozłowski, 1852). The
plaque was set up on the initiative of Eustachy Tyszkiewicz who
used an inscription from the former monument (1573) for the
plaque. However, it does not mark Vytautas' burial place, which
remains undiscovered.

Plaque commemorating
the founding of
St. Casimir's Chapel

## Chapels

An important part of the Cathedral is its chapels, particularly
St. Casimir's Chapel. They hold many historical and artistic monuments from earlier periods of the Cathedral, before Stuoka-Gucevičius rebuilt it. There are 11 chapels in the Cathedral. Walking
clockwise around the building, they are situated in the following
order: St. Ladislas' Chapel, the Wołłowicz (Royal) Chapel, the Kęsgailos Chapel, the Chapel of the Saviour's Coffin, St. Peter's Chapel,
St. Casimir's Chapel, the Bishops' Chapel, St. Ignatius Loyola's
Chapel, the Montvydai (St. Paul) Chapel, the Gasztołd Chapel and
the Chapel of the Name of the Holy Virgin Mary (Deportees). A
sacristy is situated after St. Peter's Chapel and in front of St. Casimir's Chapel.

Three-Handed
St. Casimir

St. Casimir's Chapel is one of the greatest treasures of Vilnius. It
holds the sarcophagus of the Lithuanian patron saint St. Casimir
built with an endowment from King Sigismund Vasa (1623) and
finished by his son Ladislas (1636). It is a monument of High
Baroque that hardly has any peers in this part of Europe. The
chapel was designed and decorated by Italian architects and sculptors Matteo Castello, Sebastiano Sallo and Constantino Tencalla.

St. Casimir's coffin suffered various misfortunes. When the Soviets
closed the Cathedral, it remained off-limits to believers. After
Stalin's death in October 1953 it was transferred to the Church of
St. Peter and St. Paul. On March 4th 1989 St. Casimir was ceremoniously returned to the Cathedral.

The chapel has a rectangular plan and a spacious and light cupola. Its walls are made of sandstone and lined with marble. Pink and white marble was used for decoration. The walls contain two large frescoes painted by Michelangelo Palloni in 1692: the left one represents the scene of unsealing St. Casimir's coffin and the discovery that his body that has not disintegrated in 120 years, and the right one portrays the girl Ursula's resurrection from the dead of at the holy coffin. The niches hold eight silver-plated statues of Lithuanian Grand Dukes and Polish Kings created in the 2nd quarter of the 18th cent. They apparently represent John Albrecht, Ladislas Vasa, Sigismund the Old, St. Casimir, Sigismund August, Alexander, Casimir Jagiellon and Jogaila (Jagiełło). On the east side stands a gold and silver-plated wooden Baroque pulpit representing a chalice on a spread eagle. It is traditionally related with the first rector of Vilnius University, the famous preacher Piotr Skarga, though actually it was made in the 1st half of the 18th cent. Underneath the cupola, above the door, is a loge, in which Grand Dukes and Kings, having arrived by a roofed gallery from the Lower Castle, used to listen to sermons. The wings of the cupola are decorated with frescoes and oil paintings imitating the frescoes (by Smuglevičius), and the cupola itself – with stucco works.

The stucco relief work of St. Casimir's altar, attributed to Pietro Perti (late 17th cent.), is noted for its perfect harmony. It represents the smiling Madonna with Child looking at a silver coffin of the saint carried towards her by three angels. The present coffin of the

Interior of St. Casimir's Chapel

Statue of Alexander Jagiellon in St. Casimir's Chapel. 2nd quarter of the 18th cent.

Statue of Sigismund August in St. Casimir's Chapel. 2nd quarter of the 18th cent.

Detail of the cupola of St. Casimir's Chapel

prince was made in Augsburg in 1704. On the coffin stands an expressive statuette of St. Casimir, supposedly from the 17th cent. There is also a painting representing St. Casimir dating back to ca. 1520, with silver-plated edging wrought in the 1st quarter of the 18th cent. Interestingly enough, the saint is portrayed with three hands. A legend says that the artist put a layer of paint on this extra hand, but it reappeared through the paint three times, so he left the hand where it was, considering it a miracle.

St. Casimir's Chapel is related with the tradition of Italian Renaissance by its serenity, harmony and balance, though in fact it belongs to a later period and style. Well-arranged lighting brings out its expressive forms.

The Wołłowicz (Royal) Chapel ranks second according to its artistic value; until 1636 it held the saint's coffin. It is assumed that the secret betrothal of Sigismund Augustus and Barbora Radvilaitė (Barbara Radziwiłł) took place in this chapel. The decoration of the chapel is traditionally attributed to the Dutch artist Danchers de Ry (17th cent.). Since that time it has hardly changed. Its highlights are a sumptuous Baroque altar, a cupola and frescoes.

A Classical tombstone by Mikołaj Zaleski stands out in the Kęsgailos Chapel.

A crypt underneath the Bishops' Chapel holds the remains of several Vilnius bishops, Benediktas Vaina (Benedykt Wojna), who was

Wołłowicz Chapel

Painting of the
Madonna of the
Sapiehas

considered a candidate for canonization, Stuoka-Gucevičius'
patron Ignacy Massalski and the first archbishop after the regain-
ing of independence Julijonas Steponavičius. The same crypt holds
a vessel with earth from a common grave at a Vladimir prison,
where archbishop Mečislovas Reinys martyred by the Stalinist
regime was buried.

The Gasztołd Chapel holds two earliest sculptural works in the
Cathedral: tombstones for the Great Chancellor of Lithuania
Albrecht Gasztołd and Bishop Povilas Alšéniškis (Paweł
Holszański). The first was created by Bernardo Zanobi da Gianotis
(1539–41), and the second by Giovanni Maria Padovano (ca. 1550).
These are exquisite examples of Renaissance art; Gasztołd's image

Tombstone for Albrecht
Gasztołd in the
Gasztołd Chapel

Crucifix in the Chapel
of Deportees

is massive and monumental but modelled in a realistic manner. A painting of the Madonna of the Sapiehas (16th–early 17th cent.), considered miraculous and formerly held in the Church of St. Michael, hangs is this chapel.

In the Chapel of the Name of the Holy Virgin Mary (Deportees) there is a huge wooden Baroque Crucifix (mid-18th cent.) moved from the Trinitarian Church in Antakalnis that was closed in 1864. In 1989 an inscription to commemorate the killed, imprisoned and deported during the Stalinist era, was made in this chapel. Monuments to Julijonas Steponavičius and Mečislovas Reinys have been erected here.

## The vaults

Architectural fragments, apparently the remnants of Mindaugas' first cathedral (ca. 1251) and the later pagan sanctuary (13th–14th cent.), have been discovered in the vaults. The vaults also hold the

Remains of Mindaugas' Cathedral in the vaults

Fresco "Crucified Christ with the Holy Virgin Mary and St. John"

earliest known Lithuanian fresco dating back to the late 14th or early 15th cent. It represents Christ on a cross, the Holy Virgin Mary on the right and St. John Evangelist on the left. The fresco was painted using mineral pigments and animal albumen as a binding material. It is an early Gothic work, both ascetic and decorative. It was discovered in 1985.

In 1936–39 the Royal Mausoleum holding the coffins of Alexander Jagiellon, the first wife of Sigismund Augustus, Elisabeth and Barbora Radvilaitė (Barbara Radziwiłł) was appointed underneath St. Casimir's Chapel. It also holds an urn with the heart of Ladislas Vasa.

Royal Mausoleum

Belfry

## The belfry ⑦

The belfry of the Cathedral (height – 57 m with the cross) is many-layered both from the historical and architectural viewpoint. Its foundations are superimposed on the remains of a square tower, one of the oldest brick buildings in Lithuania, whose bricks are bound in the pre-Gothic (Baltic) manner. An oval four-storey tower with loopholes was built on these remains. It is the defensive tower of the Lower Castle. The underground square part dates from the 13th cent., and the round part – from the late 14th cent. In 1522 architect Annus started the work of transforming the tower into a belfry; later more reconstructions followed. On top of the round tower three octagonal tiers were built: the first two Baroque, and the third one Classical. Regardless of this mixture of styles and epochs, the belfry looks quite uniform and harmonious. On its highest tier hangs a clock with four brass-plated faces, 2 m in diameter. The hands, figures and edgings of the faces are gilded. The clock was probably set up in the 17th cent., and its mechanism was last reconstructed in 1803. Above the clock rises a helmet-shaped roof with a spire and a cross wrought by Vilnius masters.

The belfry has 10 brass bells cast in the 16th–18th cent. by famous masters – Dutchman Jan De Lamarche, German Gustav Moerck and others. Bells toll every quarter of an hour. In 1967, 17 new bells were added.

In the direction of the castle, close to St. Casimir's Chapel, a monument to Gediminas, the founder of Vilnius, was erected in 1996. It was designed by the Lithuanian American sculptor Vytautas Kašuba and cast by sculptor Mindaugas Šnipas. In 2000 the pavement of the Cathedral Square was renewed; sites of former buildings are marked on it.

Monument to the Grand Duke Gediminas

# Pilies Street

One of the oldest streets in Vilnius, Pilies (Castle) Street started from the southern gate of the Lower Castle and led to the Town Hall. It served as a kind of spinal cord to the old town that grew

The Capitulary House (No. 4) and house No. 6

Zawadski's bookshop (No. 8)

around it. The most picturesque Vilnius lanes – Bernardinų, Šv. Mykolo, Literatų and Skapo – branch off to the right and left of Pilies Street. It has many graphic courtyards, mazy nooks and impressive buildings. The university campus is adjacent to Pilies Street on the right.

Pilies St. has always been commercial. It ends in front of the Russian Orthodox Church of St. Paraskeva and is called Didžioji from that point. This division appeared in recent times: it always used to be either one street bearing two names, or these names were used in different periods. From the crossing with Subačiaus St. Didžioji St. turns into Aušros Vartų St. All three streets form one road, around which the most interesting old town monuments are placed.

Many buildings on Pilies St. have high historical and artistic value.

No. 4 – the Capitulary House built in the 1st half of the 16th cent. Until 1939 it belonged to the capitulary of the Vilnius Cathedral. Restored in the early 17th cent. A monumental Renaissance attic (after 1616), nearly as high as the lower part of the building, is reminiscent of the attics of the Lower Castle and the Old Arsenal (reconstructed). The severe simplicity of the attic harmonizes with its decorativeness.

No. 6 – a residential house built in the late 16th – early 17th cent. and connected by an arch across Bernardinų St. with a house in front. The façade is asymmetrical, windows of the first floor have Renaissance edgings. Once there was an attic above the two-storey part, on which the present roof was built in the middle of the 18th cent.

Detail of houses No. 4 and 6 on Pilies St.

No. 8 – Zawadski's bookshop. This brick house existed since the early 17th cent., was reconstructed after the 1748 fire, and in 1800 the second floor was built on. In the 1st half of the 19th cent. a bookshop of the famous printer Józef Zawadski operated on the ground floor. Later the Blessed Bishop Jurgis Matulaitis lived on the 2nd floor. Classical elements dominate the façade, and there are some mural paintings of the same style inside the building.

No. 10 – a residential house of the early 16th cent. From 1575 it belonged to the founder of Vilnius University, Bishop Walerian

Protasewicz, and later to the capitulary of the Cathedral. In 1812 the duke and military leader Joseph Poniatowski lived there. The house has some Gothic and Classical features.

No. 12 – formerly two separate Gothic houses: the north one stood sideways to the street, and the end of the south one faced the street. Both were built before 1514 and belonged to goldsmiths, a surgeon and pharmacists; during the 1655–61 war with Moscow they were damaged and handed over to the capitulary of the Cathedral, which had them rebuilt in the Baroque style. They were severely damaged during the Second World War, renovated in 1957–60 and 1986. Decorative Gothic façades and cylindrical vaults in the basement and on the ground floor have been reconstructed.

No. 22 – the house of the Medical Collegium. A Gothic building belonging to Duke Constantine Ostrogsky and later to the great hetman of the Grand Duchy of Lithuania Christopher Radziwiłł is

Pilies Street

Bust of Juliusz Słowacki in the courtyard of house No. 22

Memorial plaque to Ferdynand Ruszczyc in the courtyard of house No. 22

Pilies St. 12

House of the Medical
Collegium (No. 22)

Hotel "Narutis"
(No. 24)

mentioned in historical sources in 1561. In 1683 the house was
bought by the university, and in the 18th cent. it was expanded and
restructured by connecting several possessions. It had an auditori-
um for medical lectures, an anatomical showroom, a chemical lab-
oratory, professors' apartments; there was a botanical garden and
a greenhouse in the courtyard. Besides other professors, this house
was home to Euzebiusz Słowacki and his son, the poet-to-be
Juliusz Słowacki. On Euzebiusz's death his widow married the
professor of medicine August Bécu. Having played a deplorable
role in the case of the Philomats, August Bécu was eventually
struck down by lightning (Adam Mickiewicz mentions this event
in *The Forefathers' Eve*). Juliusz Słowacki spent about 15 years of his
childhood and youth in this house (1811–14 and 1817–28). While
living there, he graduated from the university and wrote his first
works; his life in Vilnius is described in his later poem *An Hour of
Reflection*. A memorial plaque to the poet is set up in the courtyard,
and a niche holds his bust on a swan's wings (1927). In 1923–34
another famous Vilnius citizen – the artist, scenery designer and
public figure Ferdynand Ruszczyc, on whose initiative the bust
was built, lived in Słowacki' former apartment.

No. 24 – Hotel "Narutis". The Gothic 16th cent. house was reconstructed in the early 19th cent. and acquired some Classical features. In 1830–35 the house was home to the Polish writer Józef
Ignacy Kraszewski who drew on Lithuanian history and mythology in his writing and maintained contacts with figures of the
Lithuanian national revival movement. The house was rebuilt and
partly restructured with imitations of Gothic elements in 1967.

Courtyard of the "Victoria" house (No. 32)

Sztral's house (No. 26)

No. 26 – Sztral's house. Having acquired this house in the late 19th cent., Kazimierz Sztral reconstructed it according to architect Aleksei Polozov's project in the style of Historicism. The first floor with statues symbolizing agriculture and fishing is very decorative; niches on the second floor hold two male busts. From the late 19th cent. till 1939 the building housed the famous "White Sztral" café. On the second floor the Lithuanian Council used to hold its meetings in 1917–18. On February 16th 1918, the Act of Lithuania's Independence was signed in this building.

No. 28 – merchant Schwarz's house. The history of the building goes back to the 16th cent. Christopher Schwarz bought the dilapidated house in the mid-17th cent. Having repaired it, he sold it to the Academy, which accommodated its students there. Its next proprietor Andrzej Wiszniewski expanded the house. The present neo-Baroque façade with male and female sculptural heads dates from the late 19th or early 20th cent.

Detail of Sztral's house

No. 30 – the house of the barbers' guild (17th cent.) in the early 20th cent. belonged to Abraham Itzikovich and was renovated with his funding. The ground floor was adapted for commerce – before the Second World War Itzikovich ran an antique shop. The façade and the interiors bear distinct marks of Historicism and Modernism: particularly distinguished is a bay with high tapering windows and a balustrade.

No. 32 – the "Victoria" house. Buildings in this place are known since the 16th cent. The house acquired its Baroque appearance in the 18th cent., the façade was transformed in 1911. In the early 19th cent. it housed two wine cellars and the "Victoria" café frequented by the Philarets. Its courtyard with arches, dormer windows and an open staircase is particularly decorative and typical of Vilnius.

House of the barbers' guild (No. 30) and the "Victoria" house (No. 32)

Syrkin's house (No. 38)

No. 38 – Syrkin's house with an arch in the courtyard; from 1865 it held a bookshop, and in 1903–15 – a printing house that produced publications in the Hebrew, Yiddish, Lithuanian, Polish and Russian languages. Unfortunately, in the process of expanding his bookshop, Syrkin destroyed the Renaissance vaults of the building and unique 17th cent. mural paintings (part of them has survived on the premises of the present shop).

No. 40 – Šlapeliai house. Cultural figures of the 1st half of the 20th cent. Jurgis and Marija Šlapelis lived there. Now it houses a museum.

Šv. Jono Street

The Pharmacy house
(No. 5) and
Ertl's house (No. 7)

## Šv. Jono Street

Šv. Jono St. branches off from Pilies St. at the Church of St. John (the
buildings are numbered from Universiteto St.). One of the oldest
streets in Vilnius, it is known since the middle of the 16th cent., but
is undoubtedly older. Once the oldest Vilnius marketplace with the
first town hall was located here. Already before Lithuania's
Christianization (1386) Grand Duke of Lithuania Jogaila granted a
privilege to build the Church of St. John on this marketplace. The
most influential Lithuanian noblemen Radziwiłłs, Pacs, Sapiehas,
university professors, craftsmen and merchants lived on this street.
The university campus was formed in the course of centuries on
the north side of Šv. Jono St. In the 16th cent. nearly all houses on
this street were brick, while the street itself and quite many of its
courtyards were stone paved; some houses used to receive water
through wooden pipes from the Vingriai springs.

Strojnowski's house
(No. 9)

No. 3 – the Pac estate. The history of the building goes back to the
16th cent. Since 1628 it belonged to the Pac magnate family. In 1783
the dilapidated building was bought, renovated and decorated by
the Chancellor of the Grand Duchy Alexander Michael Sapieha.
After the suppression of the 1831 uprising, the palace that at that
time belonged to the artillery general Francis Sapieha was confiscated and handed over to the governor's office. Until the early
20th cent. a printing house that produced mainly Polish and Russian

Pac estate (No. 3)

Rusiecki's house
(No. 11)

publications operated in the palace; the first Lithuanian publication – the tsar's manifesto about the abolishment of serfdom – appeared in 1863. In 1959, 1965 and 1986 the palace was renovated. Now the building houses a community centre, a gallery, a theatre etc.

No. 5 – the Pharmacy house. Georg Schulz's pharmacy operated in this house since 1639. In 1655, during a raid by the Russians the house was burned down, and its proprietor was killed. In 1781 pharmacist Koszyk acquired the ruined building and reconstructed it. In the late 19th cent. merchant Moshe Antokolski renovated the house according to architect Aleksei Polozov's project and rendered it its present appearance. After the merchant's death in 1902, the house was parcelled out among his numerous descendants; one part was given to artist Lev Antokolski.

No. 7 – Ertl's house. The building is mentioned since the 1st half of the 17th cent.; in 1691 it was acquired and renovated by Georg Ertl, a master who was commissioned to rebuild the Church of St. John destroyed during the 1655–61 war, and who later became an elder of the stone masons' guild. The façade was reconstructed in the late 19th cent. It is trimmed with a coarse-grained stucco band; on the roof, in the middle of the façade, is a decorative pediment with a semi-round arch.

No. 9 – Strojnowski's house. Built before 1645, most probably by the master of the saddle-makers' guild Martynas Ladzikas. In the 19th cent. it belonged to the university rector Hieronim Strojnowski.

No. 11 – Rusiecki's house. Two buildings on this site are mentioned as early as 1593: one was Gothic, the other Baroque. The house acquired its present appearance, partly Baroque, partly Classical, in the late 18th – early 19th cent. From 1887 artist Bolesław Rusiecki, and later his relatives lived in this house.

No. 13 and 15/23. The Radziwiłł estate – cardinalate, whose history goes back to the 15th cent. In 1541 it was leased to Marshall Nicholas Radziwiłł the Black and later to the Radziwiłł family that ruled the palace for ca. 400 years. Only part of the original building (No. 13) has survived; another part was pulled down after the Second World War, and a new large house with a gallery along Pilies St. was built on that site.

## Universiteto Street

The western boundary of the campus goes along this street; the oldest university building with Gothic elements stands there. In front of it is a gate to the courtyard of the Presidential Palace and several interesting buildings.

No. 2/18 – the Brzostowski estate. The first building in this place is known since 1595 (part of its Gothic walls has survived). In 1667–69 a plot of land with buildings was bought by a diplomat, later the Trakai voivode Cyprian Paweł Brzostowski. He connected the remnants of buildings destroyed during a war with Moscow into one palace. In 1760 the palace became a possession of Paweł Ksawery Brzostowski who had established the famed Pawlow Republic in the vicinity of Vilnius, in Turgeliai (it was a community of peasants exempt from corvée with its own constitution, coat of arms and money, which existed 30 years). The exterior and interior of the palace was decorated by architect Martin Knackfuss in 1769. Later the palace belonged to the Samogitian elder Jokūbas

Universiteto St. 3 – the oldest university building (early 16th cent.)

Courtyard of the Alumni house (No. 4)

Brzostowski estate (No. 2/18)

Nagurskis, and in the 19th cent. to the Ogiński family. The expressive façade of the palace combines features of late Baroque and Classicism. There is a relief coat of arms of the Nagurskis family at the top of the entry tympanum.

No. 4 – Alumni house. It was the Ecclesiastical Seminary founded by Pope Gregory XII in 1582. A three-storey palace with arcades was built in 1622. The arcades look similar to the arcades in the Great (Skarga) courtyard of the university. They are reminiscent of Italian Renaissance and early Baroque. It is one of the most beautiful courtyards in Vilnius. The street façade was once decorated with frescoes – portraits of 47 popes, painted over in the middle of the 19th cent. The Alumni house was closed down in 1798, and later belonged to the university and private individuals. In the times of Soviet occupation it was abandoned, and it was not until 1984 that the building was renovated. A café was set up under the arcades. On passing through the west gate, an excellent view of the south façade of the Presidential Palace and its horseshoe-shaped courtyard is exposed.

# University ⑧

The old buildings of the university occupy a large block limited
by Pilies, Šv. Jono, Universiteto, Skapo streets and Daukanto Square. Some faculties and hostels are situated in other
areas – in Naujamiestis, Antakalnis and elsewhere. However,
the entire history of the university is associated with this old
town campus, which presently houses the rector's office, library
and lecture rooms.

The Great Courtyard

The formation of the university ensemble started in 1568, when
Bishop Walerian Protasewicz bought a two-storey Gothic house,
later occupied by the Jesuit College. In the course of time 12 buildings emerged in that area, each with several wings and situated
around 12 courtyards of varying size and shape. It is a maze where
one can roam for a long time and discover ever-new interesting
details.

## Courtyards

The Library Courtyard

The Great Courtyard is the most valuable in the historical and
artistic respect. It is decorated with arcades, and on the east closed
by the magnificent façade of the Church of St. John and a mighty
belfry. Its harmonious space reminds one of an Italian Renaissance
square, though the courtyard combines elements of three styles –
Renaissance Mannerism, Baroque and Classicism. The northern
and western buildings of the courtyard date from the late 16th
cent.; thus the courtyard itself, having been formed in the 1st half
of the 17th cent., was called the Academy Courtyard. A Classical
two-storey building with an audience chamber in its southern part
was built in 1816 and now includes a representational entry to the
university. On the façade of the Church of St. John memorial
plaques to the first rectors Piotr Skarga and Jakub Wujek, and
under the arcades – plaques with names of famous professors are
set up. On the west side there is a passage to the Observatory
Courtyard, and on the northern side – a stairway to the Sarbievijus
Courtyard. On the first floor of the north and west wall, 18th cent.
frescoes representing Bishop Walerian Protasewicz, great hetman
John Carol Chodkiewicz and King August III and Stanislaus
August Poniatowski were uncovered in 1977–79 and 1995.

The Observatory Courtyard is ringed with enclosed arcades alongside all three storeys (open arcades did not suit the northern climate of Vilnius). Its ambience is much more intimate and idyllic than that of the Great Courtyard. In the north stands a building of the old observatory with twin cylindrical towers covered with small cupolas. This monument of early Baroque was designed by Martin Knackfuss (1782–88). The building is decorated with a picturesque frieze with signs of the Zodiac and two Latin inscriptions: *Addidit antiquo virtus nova lumina coelo* (Courage gave new light to the old sky) and *Haec domus Uraniae est: curae procul este profanae! Temnitur hic humilis tellus: hinc itur ad astra* (This is the house of

Wall décor of the super-structure of the Astronomical Observatory

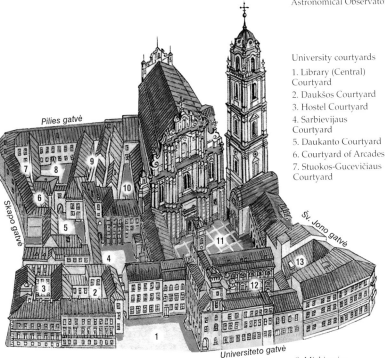

University courtyards

1. Library (Central) Courtyard
2. Daukšos Courtyard
3. Hostel Courtyard
4. Sarbievijaus Courtyard
5. Daukanto Courtyard
6. Courtyard of Arcades
7. Stuokos-Gucevičiaus Courtyard

8. Mickiewicz Courtyard
9. Stanevičiaus Courtyard
10. Sirvydo Courtyard
11. Great (Skargos) Courtyard
12. Observatory (Počobuto) Courtyard
13. Courtyard of the Printing House

Urania [i.e. the Muse of astronomy]: away, daily concerns! Here the humble earth is despised; from here to the stars). A plaque with a Polish inscription commemorating an anniversary of the Educational Committee is set up below. The oldest building of the university dating back to the 16th cent. and bought for the collegium by Bishop Protasewicz in 1568 is situated on the west side of the courtyard (holding a memorial plaque to Martynas Počobutas). It has been renovated, and on its other side facing Universiteto St. Gothic walls were uncovered in 1979.

The Library (Central) Courtyard is open and connected with Simono Daukanto Square. Like other courtyards, until the early 19th

Observatory Courtyard

cent. it was closed, and in 1825 in the process of restructuring the Governor General's office (now the Presidential Palace) that blocked the street, part of the university buildings were pulled down. In the south of the courtyard stands the Central Palace of the university built in the late 16th cent.; the third floor was built on in 1752–66 according to astronomer Tomas Žebrauskas' (Tomasz Żebrowski) project as a decorative façade of the astronomical observatory with a tower. Above the windows of the observatory planetary symbols are set up, and between the windows astronomical devices are painted (1772). The loggia of the building holds a statue of poet Kristijonas Donelaitis (sculptor Konstantinas Bogdanas, 1964). On the opposite side of the courtyard, a memorial plaque to Ukrainian poet Taras Shevchenko, who attended artist Jonas Rustemas' (Jan Rustem) studio at the university in 1829–31, is set up.

In the north the Library Courtyard connects with the Daukšos Courtyard encircled with late Classical buildings. The apartment of the professor of the painting chair Jonas Rustemas was once located in this courtyard.

From the Library Courtyard an arched passageway leads to the Sarbievijaus Courtyard. Its oldest southern building with massive two-storey buttresses was built in the 16th cent. and has underwent few changes. The courtyard is dominated by the western

Sarbievijaus Courtyard

building: decorated with arches and picturesque tiled buttresses, it was built in the 17th–18th cent. and renovated in the 1st half of the 19th cent. It housed the parsonage of the Church of St. John; today on the ground floor one finds a bookshop "Littera" decorated with frescoes by Antanas Kmieliauskas (1978), which represent professors and graduates of the old university and symbols of various sciences. On the west side of the courtyard a memorial plaque to Motiejus Kazimieras Sarbievijus is set up. The surrounding buildings house the Philological Faculty and the Centre of Lithuanian Studies. A small pool and a birch-tree render a somewhat melancholic mood to the courtyard.

Daukanto Courtyard

From the Sarbievijaus Courtyard one can walk to the Daukanto Courtyard. On its south side a nice detail of a Renaissance attic with double arches supported by high pilasters is found. A passageway in the north leads to the smallest Courtyard of Arcades renovated in 1974, a passageway in the east – to the Mickiewicz Courtyard surrounded by two-storey buildings; a Gothic façade of one of them facing Pilies St. (No. 13) is renovated. It is traditional-

Sarbievijaus Courtyard

ly assumed that the first-year student Adam Mickiewicz lived in one of those buildings, and later it became a gathering place of the Philomats.

Mickiewicz Courtyard

Two neo-Classical buildings ring the narrow Courtyard of the Printing House. A Gothic house that used to stand on this site was given to the Academy in the early 17th cent. and a formerly established printing house was moved in. In 1805 the university assigned the printing house to Józef Zawadski who published the first books by Adam Mickiewicz. In addition to the printing house, Zawadski also ran a bookshop. In 1828 tsarist authorities forced Zawadski to move out of the university building.

At Šv. Jono St. No. 2/1 (adjacent to the printing house, by Universiteto St.) in 1687 the Jesuits ran a pharmacy.

## Halls and interiors

The most interesting part of the university is the library with its many halls of high artistic value. The oldest and most impressive of these halls is the Smuglewicz Hall appointed in the 1st half of the 17th cent. It is situated on the ground floor of the eastern part of the Library (Central) Courtyard. Originally it housed a refectory, and later a hall for public lectures and a library. Franciszek Smuglewicz decorated it in 1802–04, and afterwards it became a university audience chamber. When the university was closed down, the hall held the Museum of Antiquities, and later the Vilnius Public Library. Early mural paintings were renovated in 1929. They consist of a Baroque multi-figure composition "The Holy Virgin Mary, Patron of the Jesuits" (17th cent.) in the middle part of the vaults, and Classical ornaments and busts representing men of science and art of ancient Greece painted by Franciszek Smuglewicz. The hall holds a permanent exhibition of early manuscripts and books containing many rare items, e.g. *De revolutionibus orbium coelestium* by Nicolaus Copernicus (On the Revolution of Celestial Bodies, 1543) – according to a legend, this particular copy was given to Copernicus in his deathbed, – as well as the *Catechism* by Martynas Mažvydas (the first Lithuanian book, 1547) and others.

The White Hall

Above the Smuglewicz Hall is the general reading room of the library that also dates from the times of the old academy, and on the 2nd floor – a Classical hall, so-called professors' reading room, appointed by Michael Schulz and Karol Podczaszyński in the 19th cent.

Smuglewicz Hall

The Lelewel Hall, constituting the top part of the former 18th cent. rococo chapel, also belongs to the library. Of its early décor, two angel figures and a detail of floral ornament have survived. The vaults are decorated with mural paintings by Jerzy Hoppen (1930). Part of the private library of the famous historian Joachim Lelewel is held here.

In the White Hall, an early Classical (partly Baroque) portal with relief portraits of King Stanislaus August Poniatowski and the founder of the observatory Elżbieta Puzynina should be mentioned. It is adjoined by the 18th cent. observatory decorated with symbols of constellations and other paintings. Antique astronomical devices are held there.

From the Great Courtyard one can reach a Classical audience chamber with Corinthian columns designed and decorated by Schulz and Podczaszyński. In 1929 busts of university professors created by Kazimierz Jelski (early 19th cent.) were moved to it from the Smuglewicz hall: five of them remained, others were recreated by Jonas Jagėla in 1978. Underneath the audience cham-

Lelewel Hall

ber is a students' café, and nearby – a memorial plaque for the founder of the university, King Stephen Batory. The Śniadecki (Students' Theatre) Hall with a wooden gallery and a ceiling decorated with coffers is located on the 2nd floor. It belonged to the theatre since the middle of the 18th cent.; in 1919–78 it held the university assembly hall.

In the Daukanto Courtyard, on the 2nd floor, one can see a Classical interior of architect Schulz's apartment.

There are many contemporary mural paintings, created by Lithuanian artists mainly on the occasion of the 400th anniversary of the university. The lobby of the Philological Faculty boasts the images of 9 muses and their mother Mnemosyne executed using the sgraffiti technique (art. Rimtautas Gibavičius, 1970). The reading room of the same faculty is decorated with a fresco entitled "Martynas Mažvydas in Ragainė" (art. Šarūnas Šimulynas, 1969). In the lobby of the eastern building of the Mickiewicz Courtyard there is a granite mosaic representing ancient Lithuanian and Prussian gods (art. Vitolis Trušys, 1978). Donelaitis' reading room holds paintings on the theme of Kristijonas Donelaitis and his poem *The Seasons* executed with tempera on wood (art. Vytautas Valius, 1979). The Rectorate Hall is decorated with frescoes by artist Antanas Kmieliauskas (1979–82). Particularly interesting is the interior of the Centre of Lithuanian Studies in the Sarbievijaus Courtyard: its walls and vaults are covered in original frescoes on ethnographic and mythological themes entitled "The Seasons" (art. Petras Repšys, 1976–85).

## The Church of St. John and the belfry ⑨

The Church of St. John (to be more precise, St. John the Baptist and St. John the Apostle and Evangelist) dominates the university

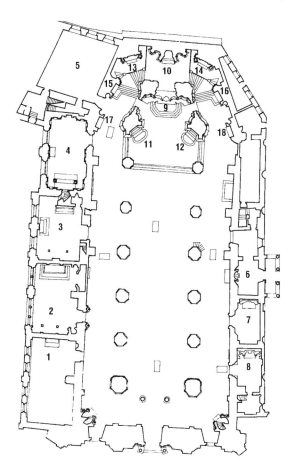

Plan of the Church of St. John

1. St. Stanislaus Kostka's Chapel
2. St. Anne's Chapel
3. Chapel of the Solace of the Mother of God
4. Ogiński Chapel
5. Sacristy
6. Narthex
7. Piasecki Chapel
8. St. Barbara's Chapel
9. High altar
10. Altar of St. Mary of Loretto
11. Altar of St. Ignatius
12. Altar of St. Xavier
13. Altar of Christ Crucified
14. Altar of the Dolorous Mother of God
15. Altar of St. Casimir
16. Altar of St. Michael
17. Altar of St. Joseph
18. Altar of St. Peter and St. Paul

ensemble. Since the times of the Jesuit Academy professors and students used to pray here, and Vilnius theologians gave sermons. It was a place for performances and disputes, where theses were defended and kings greeted. The tradition of famous preachers was not broken in later times: during Hitler's occupation, the Reverend Alfonsas Lipniūnas, who was later imprisoned by the Nazis in the Stutthof camp and perished, delivered rebellious sermons in St. John's Church. In the Soviet times the church was

Church and belfry
of St. John

closed down and severely damaged. In 1979 a university museum
was founded there. In 1991 the church was returned to its parishioners. On his visit to Lithuania in 1993, Pope John Paul II held a
meeting with intellectuals here.

The construction of the church started soon after Lithuania's
Christianization (1387) and was finished in 1426. Originally it was
Gothic: features of this style are still distinct in its interior (three
naves of equal length with 14 slender eight-plane pillars), pointed-
arch windows and massive buttresses. In 1571 the church was
taken over by the Jesuits. They built a wide Gothic presbytery with
a passage around the altar. In 1738–49 the church was reconstructed according to a project by architect Jan Krzysztof Glaubitz in a

distinct late Baroque style. During the 1827–28 reconstruction, architect Karol Podczaszyński destroyed the bulk of the sumptuous Baroque interior – nearly 3,000 carts with splinters of altars, sculptures and stucco works were taken to a dump; chapels suffered the least.

The Baroque façade designed by Glaubitz, of a symmetrical composition, rolling forms, reminiscent of a huge organ, leaves one an extraordinary impression. Its decorativeness is enhanced by cartouches, volutes, statues, metal vases and crosses. The façade is tapering, its relief gets lighter upwards thanks to a chiaroscuro effect. Nearby stands a five-tier, 63 m high belfry of a square plan (one of the highest buildings in the old town), holding decorative vases and a cross, 6,2 m high, wrought by Vilnius masters. The façade was created in the 18th cent., and the belfry – in the late 16th or early 17th cent. and heightened later; it has both Baroque and Renaissance features. The pediment of the back façade of the church facing Pilies St. also has very expressive forms (it can be best seen from the courtyard of the medical college, or Słowacki's house). It is also attributed to late Baroque. Underneath an original memorial plaque – an epitaph to the Chreptowicz family – is erect-

High altar

Statue of St. Bonaventura

Altar of St. Victor

ed (1759). Above the plaque a large cross with a human-size gilded figure of Christ used to hang.

The central focus of the church interior is a composition of 10 presbytery altars, unique in Lithuania and the Baltic countries (before Podczaszyński's "reconstruction" there were as many as 22 altars in the presbytery and naves!). It is a virtuoso Baroque work (18th cent.), called "optical music" by the art historian Mikalojus Vorobjovas. The altars are positioned in a semi-circle, on varying planes and levels, and light illuminates them through the Gothic presbytery windows. They are abundantly decorated with paintings and sculptures. The altars are counterbalanced by the organ choir with a rolling Baroque parapet. The organ of the Church of

St. John was the most famous one in Lithuania, but in the Soviet period it was destroyed; presently it has been restored. In the central nave at the pillars stand 18 sculptures, 12 of which represent various saints bearing the name of John (2nd half of the 18th cent.)

Of the chapels, the most expressive are St. Anne's and the Ogiński Chapels (both on the north side of the church). St. Anne's Chapel is noted for a sumptuous rococo portal made of red marble and stucco; plated in polychrome, gold and silver, St. Victor's altar in its central part holds the Crucifix (mid-18th cent.) surrounded by a wine tree-shaped relief work. The Ogiński Chapel seems to be the most magnificent one. Its portal is partly Baroque, with explicit features of Classicism. The portals of both chapels were created by Glaubitz. The Baroque altars of St. Barbara's and Piasecki Chapels are quite elaborate. The Ogiński Chapel contains a fresco entitled "The Life of Jews in the Wilderness", and the Chapel of the Solace of the Virgin Mary – frescoes depicting the life of St. Stanislaus Kostka. The naves and the sacristy are also covered in mural paintings. All frescoes in the Church of St. John date from the 18th cent. and were uncovered and restored in 1970's. Stained glass windows were produced in the 2nd half of the 19th – early 20th cent. in Paris and Riga. Mention should be made of the wooden Crucifix (16th cent.) supposedly donated by Piotr Skarga, Baroque pews and confessionals ornamented with carvings and inlay, and a Baroque brass bell in the belfry (1676).

The church contains many memorial monuments: to Hieronim Strojnowski (sculpt. Karol Podczaszyński and Kazimierz Jelski, 1827), Adam Mickiewicz (sculpt. Piotr Stryjeński and Marceli Gujski, 1899), Antoni Edward Odyniec (sculpt. Jan Rudnicki, 1901),

Monument to Adam Mickiewicz

Detail of the fresco in the Ogiński Chapel

Ludwik Kondratowicz-Władysław Syrokomla (sculpt. Pius Weloński and Petras Rimša, 1908), Tadeusz Kościuszko (sculpt. Antanas Vivulskis, 1917), Konstantinas Sirvydas (sculpt. Juozas Kėdainis, 1979), Simonas Daukantas (sculpt. Gediminas Jokūbonis, 1979) and others.

Skapo Street

Lopaciński or
Sulistrowski estate
(Skapo St. 4), farther –
de Reuss Palace

## Skapo Street

One of the most typical Vilnius by-streets, narrow, curved, distinguished by the interplay of light and shadows. It marks the not-
hern limit of the campus. An arch from Pilies St. leads to Skapo St.;
a nice perspective view of de Reuss palace is exposed on its opposite (west) side.

No. 4 – the Lopaciński or Sulistrowski estate. A brick house stood
on this site as early as 1545. In the late 18th cent. it was rebuilt in
the Classical style according to Martin Knackfuss' project. The
Vilnius-born prodigy violinist Jasha Heifetz probably studied
music in this house.

## Presidential Palace
## and Daukanto Square

The triangular Daukanto Square (once called Napoleon Sq., in the
Soviet times – Kutuzov Sq.) adjacent to the university and almost
connecting with the Cathedral Square, is perhaps the most beautiful and elegant in Vilnius. It is surrounded by Classical buildings
of nearly equal size on all sides except the northeast, where the
Bonifratri Church of the Holy Cross stands; it stems from an earlier period, but harmonizes well with the ensemble. Today the representational centre of the Republic of Lithuania – the Presidential
Palace – is situated in this square.

# Presidential Palace ⑩

The history of this palace (Daukanto Sq. 3) is no less complex than that of the majority of famous Vilnius buildings. It is known since the 14th cent. as a residency of the noblemen Gasztołd. In 1543 it was acquired by the Vilnius bishops who resided there until 1794. The remains of a brick building that have been discovered may belong to the earliest bishops' palace, in which Bishop Christian crowned King Mindaugas. In 1795 the palace became the headquarters of the Governor General of Vilnius. In 1800–01 and 1809–11 Governor General Mikhail Kutuzov, and in 1812 – Napoleon lived there. In 1824–32 Karol Podczaszyński reconstructed the palace according to a project by the famous Russian architect Vasily Stasov. Since the palace blocked Universiteto St., part of the university buildings standing closer to the street were pulled down.

Presidential Palace
from the park

The main façade of the
Presidential Palace

The palace has always been representational: rulers, kings and kings-to-be – Napoleon, Stanislaus August Poniatowski, Russian tsar Alexander I, King of France Louis XVIII and others – used to stay there on their visits to Vilnius. For some time the palace was a residence of Governor General Mikhail Muravyov who suppressed the 1863 uprising (in front of the palace a monument to Muravyov used to stand, and his museum was established in the corps-de-garde). Later Lucjan Żeligowski, Józef Piłsudski and presidents of Poland used to stay in the palace. The Soviets turned it into an officers' club, later to be converted into the Artists House. In 1939, when Vilnius had been returned to Lithuania, plans to settle the

Funeral of Polish legionaries in the court-yard of the present Presidential Palace. 1920. Photo by Jan Bułhak

Presidency in the palace were advanced. It was not until 1997 that these plans were carried out. Here the President performs his duties and receives foreign dignitaries. The palace façade bears the Vytis sign. When the President is in the palace, the presidential flag is raised above the Vytis.

The palace is built in the late Classical (Empire) style, monumental and solemn. Having designed many significant buildings in St. Petersburg, Stasov followed the patterns of St. Petersburg architecture here as well. The palace has 3 risalitas protruding into the

Details of the interior of the Presidential Palace

square and the courtyard. The square façade is decorated by triangular pediments, a parapet and Doric columns. Particularly elegant is the courtyard façade with an Ionic colonnade, flanked by side colonnades and a corps-de-garde (an office of guards – incidentally, the sole building with this function in Lithuania). A sizeable garden stretches out behind the palace. This regular ensemble seems to be inlaid in the chaotic mediaeval old town of Vilnius.

The interior is also very interesting – the White, Red, Green and Coffer Halls, guest rooms and a lobby. Some mural paintings have survived, and in the basement and on the ground floor one can see cylindrical vaults and other details from the early Bishops' Palace. The façade of the Presidential Chancellery is decorated in the sgraffiti technique.

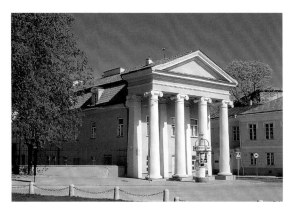

De Reuss Palace
(Daukanto Sq. 2)

## De Reuss Palace ⑪

The Palace (Daukanto Sq. 2) is a distinct partly Baroque, partly Classical monument that strikes a compositional balance to the Presidential Palace. It was built in the middle of the 18th cent. and reconstructed after 1798 (the attached four-pillar portico is attributed to architect Martin Knackfuss). The Palace had 16 large and 12 small rooms, and ancillary buildings of a horse-stable and a coach-house accommodating four carts. In the 19th cent. the proprietors of the palace were Counts de Reuss and Platers, orientalist Ignas Žiogelis (Ignacy Żagiell) and others.

Detail of the palace

## Church of the Holy Cross and the Bonifratri Monastery ⑫

On the site of the present church and monastery (Daukanto Sq. 1) Vilnius Bishop Povilas Alšėniškis built a Gothic Chapel of the Holy Cross (1543), which has survived in the eastern part of the monastery. In 1618 a two-storey house merged with the chapel. In 1635 the Bonifratri monks who had come to Vilnius converted the house into a Baroque church; it was reconstructed several times in the 18th cent. In 1976 a concert hall called the Small Baroque Hall was appointed in the church. At the present time the church is open to its parishioners.

Bonifratri Church

Monument to Laurynas
Stuoka-Gucevičius

It is the only church in Vilnius transformed from a dwelling house. With its simple forms and small mass it harmonizes with other buildings in Daukanto Sq. Late Baroque and rococo dominates in the interior. The high altar holds a painting of the Holy Virgin Mary of Snow considered miraculous; her image is duplicated on the façade fresco. A sculpture of the Crucifix distinguished among other similar sculptures in Vilnius by its extremely dark colour is also considered miraculous. The Bonifratri used to tend to sick people, thus a large part of the monastery is occupied by a spacious hospital hall with some elements of early Baroque.

In front of the church stands a monument to architect Laurynas Stuoka-Gucevičius (sculptor Vladas Vildžiūnas, 1984). In the vicinity (Stuokos-Gucevičiaus St. No. 9/7) stands a house in which a famous Vilniusite, public figure, the founder of the Library of the Academy of Sciences Tadeusz Wróblewski was born in 1858. Future leaders of the rebels Zygmunt Sierakowski, Konstanty Kalinowski, Jarosław Dąbrowski and others used to visit Wróblewski's parents in this house.

## Dominikonų Street

Dominikonų Street

One of the oldest and once most sumptuous streets in Vilnius. In the 16th cent. it was almost totally lined with brick buildings; some houses on this street used to receive water through wooden pipes from the Vingriai springs. Since olden times there were two churches on this street – a smaller Church of the Holy Trinity and a large Church of the Holy Spirit with a Dominican monastery dominating the entire block. The Institute of Piusite monks, later – the Noblemen's and Russian Girls' Institutes and boys' high schools operated on this street. Buildings on this street were home to university professors, other famous people, noblemen, among others – Michael Cleophas Ogiński, a composer and author of the famed Polonaises. Probably the most remarkable residents of the street were the Sapieha family that had two palaces there. In 1806 the first post office was opened on Dominikonų St. Dominikonų St. continues Šv. Jono St.: it connects Universiteto St. with Vilniaus and Vokiečių streets.

Church of the Holy Trinity

## Church of the Holy Trinity ⑬

On the site of the present church (Dominikonų St. 12) a Gothic single-nave church was built in the 15th cent. It was reconstructed after the 1748 and 1749 fires: a new presbytery and two towers were built on, and in place of a Gothic apse a new portal was erected. The church belonged to the university; one of its deans was the university rector, astronomer Martynas Počobutas. The tsarist authorities converted it into a Russian Orthodox church in 1821, but in 1920 it was returned to the Catholics. In Soviet times the church was abandoned. In 1968 part of the façade with a portal collapsed; in 1971 the early Gothic three-wall apse was reconstructed in that place. A 16th–18th cent. building has survived closer to Šv. Jono St.; its ground floor accommodated men's almshouse, and the first floor – a deanery. After the First World War it housed the Club of Vilnius Lithuanians and the Vilnius Union of Lithuanian Students. The building has some features of Baroque and Historicism.

Dominican Church

# Church of the Holy Spirit
## and the Dominican Monastery ⑭

The Dominican Church of the Holy Spirit (Dominikonų St. 8) is one of the most magnificent Vilnius churches, an excellent monument of high and late Baroque. Crowned with a mighty cupola, it stands out in the panorama of the old town and can be seen from surrounding streets.

It is thought that a small (probably wooden) church stood here already in Gediminas' times. In ca. 1408 Vytautas built the Church of the Holy Spirit that was later expanded. In 1501 Alexander Jagiellon gave it to the Dominican Monastery, the oldest in Lithuania. In 1679–88 it was expanded and reconstructed. The walls of the church survived from that period; the interior décor was created in 1749–70, the cupola was reconstructed in 1752–60. In 1844 the tsarist authorities closed the monastery down and the church became parochial. Today it serves the Vilnius Polish Catholic community.

Portal of the Dominican Church

The church stands sideways to the street and does not have a clearly designed main façade. Its height with the cupola is 51 m. The bottom part of the façade (with small twin towers) is covered over by monastery buildings. The exterior has features of high and late Baroque. Noted for playful rococo ornamentation, the interior of the church is one of the most valuable in Lithuania. It is heralded by the cartouches of the portal with coats of arms and fresco settings in the monastery-like corridor leading to the church.

There are 16 altars in the church. Rather massive, but dynamic and elegant, the altars make up a harmonious composition supplemented by a pulpit and a confessional (connected into one). Architectural elements and motifs, lines and volumes interact and merge

turning almost immaterial. An exceptionally original element is a rolling organ choir supported by "upturned" pillars whose bases are narrower than their capitals. The organ itself is the only surviving original 18th cent. instrument in Lithuania (master Adam Casparini).

The altars and the pulpit are lavishly decorated with round and relief sculptures and ornamentation. The church also has many Baroque frescoes; a multi-figural composition "Apotheosis of the Holy Spirit" (neo-Baroque, 19th cent.) in the cupola should be mentioned. 45 paintings in the church (an image of St. Barbara with a 17th–18th cent. setting, a rococo "St. Catherine of Siena" by Szymon Czechowicz, a portrait of Alexander Jagiellon by an unknown artist of the 2nd half of the 18th cent.) are considered monuments of art. A 20th cent. painting "Mercy of God", painted according to St. Faustine's vision by Eugeniusz Kazimirowski in 1934, is revered by pilgrims.

The right nave holds an altar in front of which Vilnius patriots are said to have prayed before starting the 1863 uprising. An entry under the altar leads to the vaults, which are labyrinthine, with many rooms and crypts, apparently of two or even more storeys. In the vaults rest ca. 2,000 mummified corpses from the 17th–18th cent. (according to some opinions, there are plague victims and Napoleon's soldiers among them).

At the church, on Šv. Ignoto St., a Dominican monastery was established in 1501. Like many others, this monastery was converted into a prison by the tsarist authorities in 1807. It was a place of

Organ of the
Dominican Church

Dominican Church
from Stiklių Street

Fresco in the cupola of
the Dominican Church

Mercy of God. 1934.
Art. Eugeniusz
Kazimirowski

imprisonment for many Lithuanian patriots – the Philarets, participants of the 1831 and 1863 uprisings. Three-storey wings of the
monastery ring a nearly square cloister, in which a shrine containing a sculpture of Mother of God on a small column was set up in
memory of plague victims in the 18th cent. (it did not survive).
Corridors are decorated with frescoes from the 18th cent.

## Estates on Dominikonų St.

No. 9 – a Historicist building with a decorative façade. A trendy
pub "Prie universiteto" now occupies the ground floor and the
courtyard.

No. 11 – the Pociej estate. Mentioned since the 17th cent., reconstructed and expanded after the 1748 fire, the palace belonged to
Trakai voivode Alexander Pociej. During Kościuszko's uprising in

Bass-relief work repre-
senting St. George on
the street façade of the
Pociej estate (No. 11)

Façade decoration of
the Pociej estate

The Górecki and
Zawisza estates
(No. 15/1 and 13)

1794, the palace served as a hideout for the last hetman of the
Grand Duchy, Szymon Kossakowski, who had sided with the
Russians; later the rebels found him in the attic and hanged him in
the Town Hall Square. In the 1st half of the 20th cent. the palace
housed Marija Šlapelienė Lithuanian bookshop frequented by
Žemaitė, Vaižgantas and other famous Lithuanian figures. The
owners not only sold, but also published books. The street and
courtyard façades contain elements of early Baroque, among them
volutes above a portal, two bass-relief works representing riders
(St. George and St. Martin), and a two-storeyed arched gallery in
the courtyard. The colour scale of the palace is typical of early
Baroque.

No. 13 – the Zawisza estate. Known since the late 16th–early 17th
cent., renovated in the late 18th cent. The façade is strictly symmetrical, done in the style of early Classicism. Renaissance vaults
have survived.

Details of the façade of
Dominikonų St. 9

No. 15/1 – the Górecki estate. A two-storey Gothic house was built
on this site in the late 15th or early 16th cent. In 1649 it was bought
by the Vilnius Academy. In the 1st half of the 18th cent. the house
was reconstructed; in 1775–90 it belonged to the regent of Grodno
Walenty Górecki who rebuilt it and turned it into a palace. Early
Classical style dominates in the building. A round tower accentu-
ates the corner (until 1950 there was a symmetrical tower on the
other side of Gaono St.).

Šv. Ignoto Street

# Šv. Ignoto Street
## and the Church of St. Ignatius ⑮

A picturesque by-street connects Dominikonų and Liejyklos streets. On its southwest side stands the Dominican Monastery, and on the opposite side – the Church of St. Ignatius and the ensemble of the Jesuit Novitiate (Šv. Ignoto St. 4, 6).

The church was built in 1622–47. Devastated by fires, in 1748–50 it was reconstructed under architect Tomas Žebrauskas. In the tsarist times it housed an officers' club and was partly destroyed; in 1925 it was returned to believers and adapted for religious needs (The Garrison Church). In Soviet times the church was turned into a film studio warehouse. The main façade with early Baroque obelisks is quite decorative and original.

The construction of the Jesuit Novitiate began in 1602–04. Its present plan and extent were formed in 1622–33. A brewery, a hospital and craftsmen workshops, in which the Russian tsar Peter I took interest on his visit to Vilnius in 1705, operated at the Novitiate.

Corner house of
Šv. Ignoto and
Benediktinių streets

Frescos on the ceiling
of the Novitiate

Šv. Ignoto Street and the Church of St. Ignatius

Rhetoric and poetics was taught. It had a rich library noted for books on ascetics. In 1798 the buildings were converted into soldiers' barracks; they were severely damaged in the 2nd half of the 19th cent. and during the Second World War. In 1985 the main part of the ensemble was renovated according to architect Evaldas Purlys' project. The most impressive part is the main building with

Detail of the fresco on the ceiling of the Novitiate

Novitiate

three-storeyed built-up arched galleries; the courtyard is separated from the street by a defensive wall with loopholes and an entry gate (from an earlier period). White arched galleries are accentuated by black decorative elements. This formerly representational part of the Novitiate now houses a library. In the 2nd (southeastern) courtyard there is a refectory: its hall extends over two storeys, and the vaults are covered with Baroque frescoes.

Monument to Jonas Žemaitis

A house of nobleman Kęsgaila from Vytautas' milieu is probably incorporated into the Benedictine convent marked as Šv. Ignoto No. 7 (though this is not definitely proved). Gothic forms have been uncovered on the street façade.

On the east side of the Novitiate facing Totorių St. stands the Ministry of Defence. In front of it a bust of the guerilla general Jonas Žemaitis (1909–54) is erected (sculptor Gintautas Lukošaitis, 1999). After the Second World War the artillery officer of independent Lithuania Jonas Žemaitis became the chairman of the Lithuanian Freedom Movement, was arrested in 1953, interrogated by the head of the Soviet KGB Lavrenty Beria and shot in Moscow.

Radziwiłł estate

Memorial plaque to the
rescuers of Jews in the
courtyard of Šv. Ignoto
St. 5

Houses on Liejyklos
Street

Liejyklos St. 1

## Estate of Janusz Radziwiłł and Liejyklos Street ⑯

On the north Šv. Ignoto St. connects with Liejyklos St., where masters who used to cast bells for Vilnius churches once lived. West of
this place, on the corner of Liejyklos St. and Vilniaus St, a palace of
Nicholas Radziwiłł the Black stood in the 16th cent. In the 2nd
quarter of the 17th cent. Janusz Radziwiłł, a famous figure of the
Grand Duchy, built a luxurious Renaissance-style residence on that
site. Its image survived on a medal coined by German medalist
Sebastian Dadler in 1653. The building had a horseshoe-shaped
plan, 5 three-storeyed pavilions and magnificent halls. The palace
boasted rich art collections containing works by famous Flemish
and Dutch artists. After the 1655–61 war with Moscow and the
Northern War (early 18th cent.) the building deteriorated. Dominik
Radziwiłł gave it to the Vilnius Welfare Society. During the First
World War the building was ruined; the western pavilion (Vilniaus
St. 22) was reconstructed as late as 1984, and since 1990 it houses a
gallery of foreign art. The building has Renaissance forms and
Mannerist décor. The east wing with a typical portal is still waiting
for renovation.

From 1915, a Jewish theatre – the ancestor of the presently widely
known theatre "Habima" in Israel – operated at Liejyklos 4. On the
corner of Šv. Ignoto and Benediktinių streets stood the house of the
chief council of rabbis, where Theodor Herzl, the founder of the
Jewish national movement (Zionism), met with the Vilnius Jewish
community in 1903. This event is commemorated by a memorial
plaque. On the other side of Benediktinių St., in the courtyard of
the Benedictine convent, stands a building of the former Ecclesiastical Archive. During the Nazi occupation one of many Lithuanians who were saving Jews, the Reverend Juozas Stakauskas,
worked there.

In front of Janusz Radziwiłł's estate, at Liejyklos St. 1, in 1966 and
later the Russian poet and Nobel prize winner Joseph Brodsky
used to read his poems to his Vilnius friends. In 2000 a memorial
plaque was set up on the house.

Church of St. Anne

## Church of St. Anne ⑰

The Church of St. Anne (Maironio St. 8) is probably the most famous structure in Vilnius. It is a masterpiece of late (so-called flamboyant) Gothic, nearly unsurpassed in the world. According to the latest data, it was designed (1495–1500) by Benedikt Rejt, an architect of the Jagiellons, who also designed Ladislas' Hall in Hradčany in Prague. It has survived into our days almost unchanged (only its surroundings were transformed when a street was laid out in front of its façade in 1869–70). The church was renovated in 1902–09, and the façade was reinforced in 1960–70.

Many legends are related with this church. Particularly popular is a story that on seeing St. Anne's, Napoleon wanted to put it on his palm and carry it over to Paris. Actually, he used the church for the needs of the French cavalry.

Detail of the door of the Church of St. Anne

A surprisingly light, harmonious and graceful building, it is noted for a rhythmical composition of vertical and curved lines: no solid masonry is placed above the portal, only pilasters, slender quadrangular poles, arches of three types (semi-round, several concave and several pointed), and elegant pinnacled towers crowned with metal crosses. Bricks of 33 varieties were used for decoration. In the opinion of art scholar Vladas Drėma, the early Lithuanian coat-of-arms – Gediminas Columns – are accentuated in the façade

Church of St. Anne

composition. Side façades and the presbytery are also very intricate, with high pointed-arch windows, buttresses and open-worked towers.

The interior of St. Anne's does not equal its ingenious and flamboyant exterior. Altars are Baroque, and the vaults are from the early 20th cent. A neo-Gothic belfry designed by Nikolaj Chagin (1873), stands near the church, and behind the belfry – a Baroque Chapel of Scala Christi (1617, reconstructed in 1820) that belongs to the ensemble of the Bernardine Church.

Detail of the high altar of the Bernardine Church

## Church of St. Francis and St. Bernardine ⑱

The Church of St. Francis and St. Bernardine, or the Bernardine Church (Maironio St. 10) is one of the largest Gothic sacral buildings in Vilnius: it acquired some features of Renaissance and Baroque in the 17th–18th cent. Being much larger and more archaic than the church of St. Anne, it forms an interesting and unique ensemble with the latter.

After their arrival in Vilnius, Bernardine monks built a wooden church in the 2nd half of the 15th cent., and at the end of the same cent. – a brick one. In the early 16th cent. it was reconstructed, apparently with the participation of a master from Gdańsk (Danzig) Michael Carpentarius. Afterwards it was renewed many times, particularly after the 1655–61 war with Moscow, when the Cossacks ravaged the church killing the monks and citizens who had taken shelter there. In the times of the Soviet occupation it was closed down and handed over to the Art Institute. In 1994, the brethren of St. Francis returned to the church, and presently it is under restoration.

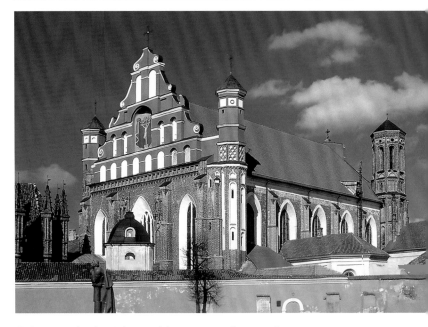

Gothic pointed-arch windows and buttresses stand out on the façade. Above them rises a pediment with twin octagonal towers on the sides and a fresco depicting the Crucifix (artist Kanuty Rusiecki, ca. 1846) in the middle niche. A Gothic presbytery is the oldest part of the church. An important accent of the exterior is a slender but not very tall octagonal tower of the belfry echoed by twin also octagonal towers on the façade. Geometrical brick ornaments add to its decorativeness.

Bernardine Church

However, the most valuable, though not yet fully restored, part is the church interior. 8 high pillars divide it into 3 naves; in the lateral naves Gothic rib-and-panel and ribbed vaults have survived. The narthex also has rib-and-panel vaults. The walls of the naves are decorated with Gothic polychrome frescoes, partly uncovered in 1981 – dynamic, colourful figural compositions on biblical and hagiographic themes, with occasional inscriptions in Gothic characters, floral ornaments, heraldic insignia etc. These mural paintings date from the early 16th cent. and are considered unique in the world: their composition and type of presentation of the subject matter belongs to Renaissance, and the stylistics – to the Gothic style.

Portal of the Bernardine monastery

11 altars of the central nave constituted a beautiful ensemble (only the high altar has survived; others are under reconstruction). All the altars are made of wood, late Baroque, of natural colour. There is also a pulpit of similar forms and sculptural décor. The whole ensemble was created in the middle of the 18th cent. The church holds the oldest known sculpture of the Crucifix in Lithuania (15th cent.) of a high artistic quality. Particularly valuable are two marble tombstones: a Renaissance one for Stanislaus Radziwiłł in the north nave, the oldest professional memorial round-sculpture composi-

Details of the interior of
the Bernardine Church

tion in Lithuania (Wilhelm van den Blocke's workshop in Danzig,
1618–23), and a Baroque one for Piotr Wiesiołowski in the south
nave (1634).

The Bernardine monastery north of the church, built simultane-
ously with the church, was renovated and reconstructed several
times. Since its founding, a novitiate and a seminary operated at
the monastery, a rich library had been accumulated, and a scripto-
rium operated. There were craftsmen, artists and organists among
the monks. The monastery won the greatest fame for preachers

Courtyard of the
Bernardine Church

who attracted large audiences (among other languages, sermons were delivered in Lithuanian). The monastery was closed in 1864, and the building housed soldiers' barracks. In 1919 it was given to the art faculty of the university, later – to the Art Institute (now the Art Academy).

Gothic forms have survived quite well on the south wall of the cloister. It is the oldest brick building of the entire complex (the church and the monastery were built later). A sacristy of the Bernardine Church with remarkable rib-and-panel vaults was also erected. Attention should be drawn to a 16th cent. portal of the sacristy, a sumptuous 15th cent. wrought metal door and fragments of 16th cent. mural paintings. Corridors and other premises are covered in rib or cross vaults.

South of the ensemble of St. Anne and Bernardine Churches, close to the Vilnia, a monument to Adam Mickiewicz was erected in 1984 (sculptor Gediminas Jokūbonis, 1980). Relief plaques on the themes of *The Forefathers' Eve*, made by Polish sculptor Henryk Kuna in 1930's, are set up around the monument. It is in this place that the first meetings of Vilnius dissidents, which gave an impetus to the independence movement, took place in 1987.

Bernardine Church from Sereikiškių Garden

Monument to Adam Mickiewicz

Between the Gothic ensemble and the Vilnia, a sizeable area is occupied by an old Sereikiškių (Bernardinų) Garden, above which loom the Hills of Bekesh and Three Crosses.

Church of St. Archangel
Michael

Detail of the vault

# Church of St. Archangel Michael and the Bernardine Convent ⑲

It is a unique Renaissance ensemble (Šv. Mykolo St. 9), which forms a beautiful counterpart to the Gothic of the Churches of St. Anne and Bernardines.

In 1594–97 the church was commissioned by the Chancellor of the Grand Duchy Leo Sapieha as a mausoleum for his family. The construction was finished in ca. 1604, but in 1627 the roofing fell in; later stonemason Jonas Kajetka rebuilt it. During the 1655–61 war with Moscow the Cossacks burned down and ravaged the church; it was renovated in 1663–73. A Baroque belfry was built in the 1st quarter of the 18th cent. The church was closed down by the tsarist authorities in 1888, and in 1905 returned to the Sapiehas who had it renovated in 1905–12. In 1933 both the church and monastery were renovated again (under supervision by Stanisław Lorentz). Since 1956 the church houses the Museum of Architecture.

The harmonious whitewashed façade of St. Michael presents a sharp contrast to the elaborate, decorative redbrick façade of St. Anne's. It is built in a transitional style from Renaissance into Baroque; there are twin towers with elegant Baroque spires on both

Epitaph to Casimir
Sapieha

Tombstone for Leo
Sapieha

Fragment of the
entablature

sides. The façade is divided by pilasters with original capitals decorated with floral motifs; the pediment has a frieze, also with floral motifs. Atop the belfry sits an iron weathervane (18th cent.) representing St. Archangel Michael crushing the devil underfoot.
Attention should be drawn to a late Classical fence, arches and
columns in the churchyard.

The interior is rich but austere. It is a single-nave space with tun-
nel vaults (in a pattern of stars, hearts and rosettes). The high altar
is of the late Renaissance style (1st half of the 17th cent.), made of
black, red, brown, dark green marble, decorated with white
alabaster; side altars are rococo (18th cent.). At the south wall, close
to the high altar there is a tombstone for Leo Sapieha and his two
wives, the largest memorial monument in Lithuania with features
of Baroque and Mannerism (4th decade of the 17th cent.). It is decorated with excellent allegoric sculptures and crowned with a statue of Christ Resurrected. A relief work on the 2nd floor depicts the
fear of the guards of Christ's grave at the Saviour's resurrection.
Relief images of Sapieha and his wives are taken from an earlier
monument (apparently intended for the Cathedral in the early 17th
cent.). A tombstone for Stanislaus Sapieha (1638–43) framing the
sacristy door is noted for its innovatory structure and symbolism.

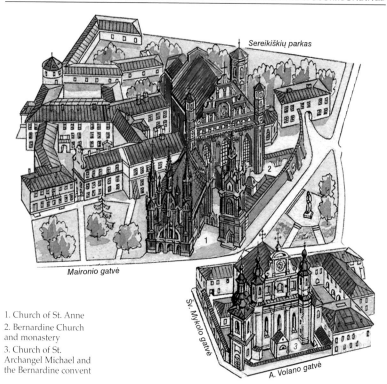

*Sereikiškių parkas*

*Maironio gatvė*

*Šv. Mykolo gatvė*

*A. Volano gatvė*

1. Church of St. Anne
2. Bernardine Church and monastery
3. Church of St. Archangel Michael and the Bernardine convent

Southeast wing of Bernardine convent

A monument to Theodore Christine Sapieżyna (architect Giovanni Battista Grisleni, sculptor Francesco de Rossi, 6th decade of the 17th cent.) stands at the south wall. All these monuments are made of marble and alabaster. The crypt of the church holds the remains of some of the Sapiehas, the founder of the church among them.

The Bernardine convent is a Renaissance building (16th–17th cent.). Its oldest and most interesting part is the southeast wing (facing the Vilnia) with massive buttresses connected with masonry at the bottom. Before a new street (now Maironio) was laid, the territory of the convent had stretched out to the Vilnia.

## Volano and Šv. Mykolo streets

On Volano St., in front of the Church of St. Archangel Michael, stands a building of the Collegium of Chemistry (No. 2/7). In the middle of the 16th cent. a house of nobleman Hornostaj, which later belonged to Nicholas Radziwiłł the Brown, stood on this site. In 1577 Radziwiłł the Brown donated it to the community of Evangelical Reformers who used it as their prayer house. In 1639 the prayer house was partly destroyed by Catholics who accused Evangelical Reformers of having fired at the Church of St. Archangel Michael; in 1641, to avoid such clashes, it was moved outside the city wall. The reconstructed palace housed the Collegium of

Courtyard of the Church of St. Archangel Michael

Chemistry in 1804; Jędrzej Śniadecki and Franciszek Smuglewicz lived and worked there. In 1924 it was given to the Educational Board, and before the Soviet-German war – to the Ministry of Education, which presently occupies the building. The palace is built in the late Classical and neo-Classical style and has a round domical hall, in which Jędrzej Śniadecki used to deliver lectures on chemistry.

Šv. Mykolo St. reaches Pilies St. in the west. Its distinctive appearance goes back to the 16th cent. A typical house of a well-off citizen (No. 8) of the late 18th–early 20th cent. contains fragments of Gothic masonry; in the 16th cent. furnaces for firing tiles operated in this house.

Cellar of house No. 8 on Šv. Mykolo St.

Russian Orthodox
Church of the Blessed
Mother of God

Detail of Gothic masonry
of the church

# Russian Orthodox Church
# of the Blessed Mother of God ⑳

This Russian Orthodox church (Maironio St. 12) stands on the left
bank of the Vilnia, close to the ensemble of the Churches of St. Anne
and Bernardines. Its cube-like volume and cupola dominate in the
valley. According to tradition, it was endowed by Juliana,
Algirdas' wife and Jogaila's mother, who was buried there. In 1415
the church was transformed into a cathedral. In 1511–22 it was
reconstructed by Prince Constantine Ostrogsky. In 1516 Helen,
wife of Alexander Jagiellon (like Juliana, she was a Russian
Orthodox), was buried there. In 1609 the cathedral was given to the
Uniates. In 1808 the desolated church, transferred to the possession
of the university, housed an anatomy showroom, a library, lecture
rooms, and a museum. In 1865–68 architects Alexander Riazanov
and Nikolaj Chagin rendered it its present appearance, and it
began to function as a church again.

Fragments of Gothic masonry have survived in the bottom part
and in some segments up to the top. The present façades and the
cupola imitate Georgian mediaeval architecture. The interior was
appointed during the reconstruction; it boasts a harmonious and
magnificent iconostasis.

Monument to
Mieczysław Dordzik

Close to the church, at the Vilnia, stands a small monument to
Mieczysław Dordzik, a pupil of the crafts school who perished
during the 1931 flood while trying to save a Jewish boy Chackel
Charmac. The monument was built by joint efforts of the Christian
and Jewish communities in 1933.

Bernardinų Street

Detail of the portal of
Bernardinų St. 6

## Bernardinų Street

Along with Skapo St., it is the most picturesque Vilnius street with
interesting perspectives. This short (250 m), narrow and crooked
lane lined with Baroque and Classical houses is surrounded by
curving walls, ancient façades and typical 17th–18th cent. courtyards. An arch spans it on the west side. Bernardinų St. connects
the ensemble of the Churches of St. Anne and Bernardines with Pilies St. In 16th cent. it was a section of a road connecting the complex of castles with the Bernardinų Gate of the city defensive wall.

Nearly all houses on this street are monuments of architecture and
history. Some of them should be mentioned in particular:

Street façade and
the courtyard of
Bernardinų St. 11

The Olizar, or Lopaciński
estate (No. 8/8)

No. 8/8 – the Olizar, or Lopaciński estate. A small brick house was
built on this site in the 1st half of the 17th cent., and the entire
ensemble expanded until the middle of the 18th cent. Michael
Lopaciński bought the house in 1762, and commissioned reconstruction according to a design by Jan Krzysztof Glaubitz, who
turned it into a magnificent palace with a semi-closed courtyard. In
1819–28 the estate belonged to Count Olizar's family, later to the
printer Zawadski. The ensemble consists of a palace with a wing,
servants' house, a maintenance building and fences with gates.
The architecture is late Baroque with some elements of Classicism.
The building has a Baroque stepped tiled roof. Particularly inter-

Courtyard of
Bernardinų St. 5

Literatų Street

Piasecki house
(Literatų St. 5)

esting is the first floor covered in a dark textured plaster, which creates a contrasting background for the white window borders and ledges. The most ornate façade with a two-storeyed window arcade faces the courtyard. The servants' house (on the corner of Šiltadaržio St.), imitating the style of the palace, was built on in the 2nd half of the 19th cent.

No. 11 – a house where Adam Mickiewicz lived. Built in the 1st half of the 17th cent. Its present appearance was formed in the late 18th cent. A closed Classical courtyard is surrounded by two-storey buildings. It has a wooden gallery; a relief work representing a lion's head is set up on the entry arch. Having arrived from Kaunas, the poet lived there in April–June 1822, wrote and edited the poem *Gražyna*. His apartment is located on the left side of the ground floor. The Mickiewicz Museum operated in this house since the 2nd half of the 19th cent., was reopened in 1955 (on the occasion of the poet's 100th anniversary of death) and renewed in 1983. One can see pieces of furniture and objects used by Mickiewicz, a registry of students of Vilnius University containing Mickiewicz's name, and artworks related to Mickiewicz.

## Literatų Street

This by-street branches off from Pilies St. and goes in a broken line towards the Church of St. Archangel Michael. In the 19th cent. there were many bookshops and antique dealers on this street, hence its name.

No. 5 – the Piasecki house built in the late 18th cent. In 1823, having arrived from Kaunas, Adam Mickiewicz resided here at the invitation of the parents of his friend Kazimierz Piasecki. The windows of his room faced the street, but its exact location is not known. Mickiewicz is thought to have written *Gražyna* and the 2nd and 4th parts of *The Forefathers' Eve* in this house; the Philomats used to gather at his place. On the pediment of the entry arch a memorial plaque with a Polish inscription is set up; plaques with Lithuanian and Russian inscriptions are set below on both sides of the arch.

## Church of Blessed Mary the Comforter and the Augustine Monastery ㉑

These buildings are monuments of late Baroque. The church (Savičiaus St. 15) is the last Baroque church built in Vilnius by an unknown architect in 1746–68. The monastery buildings facing Savičiaus, Bokšto and Augustijonų streets date from the late 18th cent. The Augustines established themselves on this site after the 1655–61 war. In 1833–42 the monastery housed the Vilnius Spiritual Academy; one of its professors was the bishop and writer-to-be Motiejus Valančius. In 1859 it was converted into a Russian Orthodox Church of St. Andrew; a painting of Blessed Mary the Comforter considered to be miraculous, along with other liturgical objects, was moved to the Church of St. John (its present location is unknown). The organ and a portrait of the founder of the Augustine Monastery, Grand Duke Vytautas, was moved to the Cathedral (now the portrait hangs above a memorial plaque to

Augustine Church and monastery

Tower of the Augustine Church

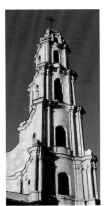

Vytautas in the Cathedral). In 1918 the church was returned to the Catholics and renovated. After the Second World War the interior was destroyed during the installation of a ferro-concrete ceiling; it was used as a warehouse. At the present time the church remains closed. Its dynamic and harmonious five-tiered tower (41.5 m) stands out in the city silhouette. A church with a single front tower is rare in Lithuanian Baroque architecture; only the Kaunas Town Hall has a similar structure.

M.K. Čiurlionis' House (Savičiaus St. 11)

## M. K. Čiurlionis' House ㉒

This building at Savičiaus St. 11 acquired its present appearance in the 18th cent. (the façade belongs to the 19th cent.) Until the middle of the 19th cent. it was home to Vilnius governors and burgomasters. In 1907–08 the world-famous artist and composer Mikalojus Konstantinas Čiurlionis lived in this house. At that time he created his most remarkable paintings. It is thought that after the opening of the 2nd exhibition of Lithuanian art his future wife, the writer Sofija Kymantaitė visited this house for the first time.

In 1995, on the artist's 120th anniversary, a memorial culture centre was opened in this house.

## Didžioji Street

It is a continuation of Pilies St. merging with the Town Hall Square
and turning into Aušros Vartų St. Didžioji St. was a centre of self-
government and commerce of old Vilnius. Mediaeval streets of
Lataiko, Bokšto and, further up – Išganytojo, branch off from a
small square at the beginning of Didžioji St., in front of the Church
of St. Paraskeva.

Interior ot the
Chodkiewicz estate
(Didžioji St. 4)

Frank's house
(Didžioji St. 1/2)

Chodkiewicz estate

No. 1/2 – Frank's house. It is an estate of Bishop Wołłowicz reconstructed after the 1610 fire (the building facing Didžioji St. dates
from the 17th cent.). In 1804 all the buildings belonged to the university and were converted into professors' apartments. Many culture figures lived there: outstanding medical doctor Józef Frank
(1804–23), chemist Jędrzej Śniadecki (1823–38), philosopher Lev
Karsavin (in 1940's), who perished in a Stalinist concentration

camp, and others. During the 1812 war the treasury of Napoleon's army was kept here; an army intendant Henri Beyle (who later became the writer Stendhal) also stayed in this building. Now it houses the French Embassy.

Courtyard of the Chodkiewicz estate

No. 4 – the Chodkiewicz estate. Formed in the period of Gothic and Renaissance, the present building is late Classical. The family of the noblemen Chodkiewicz bought a house that stood on this site in 1611 and 1619, and transformed it into a Renaissance residence. In 1834 the building was reconstructed and acquired its present appearance. In 1919 it was given to the university and was home to the professors: historian Ignas Jonynas, philosopher Vosylius Sezemanas, biologist Pranciškus Šivickis, psychologist Jonas Vabalas-Gudaitis and others. The façade is symmetrical, harmonious, moderately decorated; the façades of the servants' house facing the courtyard and Bokšto St. (No. 5) are designed in the same style. Now the palace houses the Vilnius Picture Gallery.

No. 7 – the Pac estate. In the 16th cent. two houses stood on this site; one of them was called Vytautas' House. In the 2nd half of the 17th cent. hetman Michael Casimir Pac (founder of the Church of St. Peter and St. Paul) bought a plot of land and built on a sumptuous palace apparently decorated by the same artists who had worked in the church. King Jan Sobieski, tsar Alexander I and Napoleon visited the estate on various occasions. The building was reconstructed in 1839–41. The present façade is Classical.

No. 10 – a house of the University Clinic. A Gothic palace that belonged first to the Gasztold family, and since the 16th cent. to the Radziwiłłs, used to stand there. The university bought the palace in 1824 and converted it into a clinic.

Pac estate (Didžioji St. 7)

Detail of the decoration of the Didžioji St. 5

No. 17/1 – a house on the site of the former Russian Orthodox Resurrection Church. A Gothic church was built there in the 16th cent.; part of the cellars and a refractory wall of the former building has survived. The outline of the former church except for the roof can be traced. At the present time it houses the Lithuanian Genocide and Resistance Research Centre.

No. 19/2 – Bildziukevičius' house. Built in the late 16th or early 17th cent., it belonged to the governor of Vilnius Mykolas

House of the University
Clinic (Didžioji St. 10)

Bildziukevičius. It has some Renaissance features; particularly interesting is an arched gallery in the courtyard. At the present time it houses the restaurant "Amatininkų užeiga".

Nearby, on Stiklių St. (No. 4), stands another typical building with a so-called Courtyard of the Printing House. Its history goes back to the 15th cent. It is thought that in the 16th cent. it held the Mamonichi printing house. A Gothic building in the courtyard with the façade and fragments of the interiors was reconstructed in 1974. In front of it a sculpture of "The Chronicler" is erected (sculptor Vaclovas Krutinis, 1973).

No. 25 – Antokolski's house. Built in the late 15th cent. and recon-

Wall of the former
Russian Orthodox
church in house
No. 17/1

Didžioji St. 17/1

structed several times, it belonged to the famous sculptor Mark Antokolski (1843–1902) who lived mainly in Western Europe and stayed at this house on his brief visits to Vilnius. In 1903 a monument to Catherine II designed by him was erected in the city. On the entry gateway hangs a memorial plaque from 1906 claiming that the sculptor was born there, which does not correspond to the truth – he was born in another house on Subačiaus St. that did not survive.

No. 27 – the Trinitarian house that belonged to the Trinitarian Monastery in Antakalnis. Built in the 16th–17th cent. and reconstructed after the 1748 fire, it has some elements of Gothic, Renaissance and late Classicism (a detail of Gothic masonry has been uncovered on the left side of the ground floor). Now it houses a bookshop decorated by Petras Repšys in 1978; a brass plaque

repeats the title page and a fragment of the rhymed foreword from the Catechism by Martynas Mažvydas.

No. 24 and 26 – a complex of guild houses. The Small Guild (No. 26) is one of the oldest Gothic buildings in the Town Hall Square dating from the 15th cent. In 1608 merchants rented and reconstructed the house; later it was repeatedly rebuilt and has been recently renovated. Gothic windows and entry arches have been reconstructed on the courtyard façade; the basements contain fragments of cross vaults, Gothic fireplaces and mural paintings. The Merchants' Guild (No. 24) was built in the early 16th cent. and later rebuilt with elements of early Classicism; on the main façade a fragment of a Renaissance sgraffiti ornament has survived. Gothic pediments of the Small Guild and another adjacent house can be seen in the garret.

Courtyard of the Printing House (Stiklių St. 4)

Houses on Didžioji St. (from right to left): No. 19/2, 21, 23, 25, 27

Buildings of the Guild (Didžioji St. 24, 26)

Russian Orthodox
Church of St. Paraskeva

## Russian Orthodox Church of St. Paraskeva ㉓

The Russian Orthodox Church of St. Paraskeva (Piatnica) (Didžioji St. 2) stands on a triangular square where Pilies St. turns into Didžioji St. According to tradition, a church was built on the site of a pagan sanctuary of god Ragutis in 1345. It burned down, and was replaced by a brick church in the late 16th cent. In 1611 the church and adjacent buildings with an asylum were given to the Uniates. However, the buildings were neglected: documents testify that the church was turned into an inn, and the asylum – into a brothel. It was not until the 1655 occupation that the reconstruction of the building began. In 1705 and 1708 tsar Peter I visited the renovated church and honoured it by donating flags seized from the vanquished Swedes. Probably because of this great attention to a small church a rumour spread (also confirmed by a marble plaque) that in 1705 Peter I baptized the forefather of Alexander Pushkin, the African Hannibal, in this church. In the 19th cent. the church nearly collapsed. After the 1863 uprising, when Russification was in full swing, hundreds of desolated churches were reconstructed and new ones were built in Lithuania; many Catholic churches were converted into Russian Orthodox. Particularly notorious for this activity was Governor General Mikhail Muravyov who demanded that churches similar to those found in Russia be built in Vilnius. In 1864 a neo-Byzantine church, much larger than the former one, was built on this site according to a project by architect Nikolaj Chagin.

Russian Orthodox
Church of St. Michael

## Russian Orthodox Church of St. Michael ㉔

The church stands farther apart from the street pavement (Didžioji St. 12). It was built in 1514 by the great hetman of the Grand Duchy Constantine Ostrogsky; in 1609–1827 it belonged to the Uniates. In the 18th cent. fires destroyed the old Gothic church; it was reconstructed in the late Baroque style, apparently with the participation of architect Jan Krzysztof Glaubitz. While implementing the tsarist Russification program, by Muravyov's order it was reconstructed in the Russian Byzantine style in 1865 (a plaque to Muravyov is still set up on a chapel wall). At that time a house that separated the church from the street was pulled down. The walls of the church are built in the Gothic manner, the façade and the interior has numerous Gothic details.

Nearby stands a house in which a famous Russian actor Vasily Kachalov was born in 1875 (his father was a priest of the church). Kachalov received the first lessons of his profession in high school, and later at a theatre in Vilnius.

## Church of St. Casimir and the Jesuit Monastery ㉕

The ensemble is located on the east side of the Town Hall Square (Didžioji St. 34). The construction of the church began in 1604 in memory of the holy prince Casimir: it was built by the Jesuits with funding by the Great Chancellor of the Grand Duchy Leo Sapieha. It is traditionally assumed that the corner stone (which can be seen on the façade wall) was pulled into the city by a procession of 700 Vilniusites from the Antakalnis hills. The construction was finished in 1616, and the interior design completed in 1618. The Church of St. Casimir is one of the earliest exemplary Baroque buildings in

Cupola of the Church of St. Casimir

Church of St. Casimir

Cartouche of the portal

the city, designed along the line of the famous Il Gesù church in Rome. It was apparently designed by Povilas Bokša (Paweł Boksza), and the construction was supervised by Jan Frankiewicz, a pupil of architect Giovanni Mario Bernardoni. In the middle of the 18th cent. the church was reconstructed by architect Tomas Žebrauskas. Under his supervision a stepped lantern cupola with a crown was erected. This large and impressive cupola is unique in the entire region of the former Grand Duchy. There are good grounds for thinking that the author of the project was Jan Krzysztof Glaubitz. During the reconstruction the church was magnificently decorated. In 1812 it was partly destroyed by

Interior of the Church
of St. Casimir

Šv. Kazimiero Street

Napoleon's army: the altars and part of paintings, sculptures and
furnishings were torn down, and the church was transformed into
a granary. After the 1830–31 uprising it was converted into a
Russian Orthodox church and rather unsuccessfully altered. In
1864–68 the church was turned into the Cathedral of St. Nicholas
according to a project by Nikolaj Chagin: the height of the towers
was reduced, they were topped with onion domes, and the interi-
or was reconstructed. Sources testify that during his visit to
Vilnius, Fedor Dostoyevsky prayed in this church. In 1917 the
Church of St. Casimir was returned to the Catholics, but was damaged again during the Second World War, closed down and in 1961
converted into a Museum of Atheism. It was not until 1989 that the
museum was eliminated and the building given back to parishioners, and the church was reconsecrated in 1991.

The longitudinal and transverse naves of the church form a Latin
cross. Atop rises a magnificent cupola decorated with 18th cent.
rococo ornaments. Light reaches the spacious interior through the
windows of the cupola. On the exterior the cupola has a stepped
form that appeared after the 18th cent. reconstruction. Atop the
cupola, in place of a Russian Orthodox onion dome, a crown was
reerected in 1942 (architects Vytautas Landsbergis-Žemkalnis,
Jonas Mulokas).

An exceptional feature of the interior is an excellently ordered
space. There are three decorative and elaborate late Baroque altars
created by Tomas Žebrauskas and, apparently, sculptor Jan
Nieziemkowski in 1749–55. The altars hold new paintings from the
last decade of the 20th cent.

Next to the church stands a house of the professed Jesuits, the prin-
cipal structural unit of the Jesuit province. The head of the

province lived in this house. The construction of the monastery dates from 1604–15. It housed a library, a hospital; it was home to many famous figures of the Jesuit order: architect Povilas Bokša, the saint Andrew Bobola, Konstantinas Sirvydas, Albertas Koja-lavičius-Vijūkas. The first Vilnius Lithuanian high school operated in these buildings (1915–19). At the present time the Church of St. Casimir and the house of the professed Jesuits are once more run by the Jesuits. In addition to religious services, concerts are held in the church. Part of the house of the professed Jesuits is given to the Vilnius Jesuit high school, and in the monks' old house rooms for monks are laid out.

## Town Hall ㉖

A two-storey building in the style of High Classicism stands in the centre of the Town Hall Square (Didžioji St. 31). The Town Hall was established by Jogaila's privilege in the late 14th cent.; there is a room on the east side of the cellar that may date back to the times of Jogaila or even earlier. The Town Hall was the main municipal office. In the late 16th – early 17th cent. it was Gothic; its ensemble included guards' and governors' houses, and shops under lease; a pillory and a gallows stood nearby. In the middle of the 18th cent. after a fire the building was reconstructed by Jan Krzysztof Glaubitz and Thomas Russeli; among other things, an octagonal

tower with a clock, bells and a weathervane in the shape of the Vytis were rebuilt. Before long the tower collapsed. In 1785–99 the Town Hall was rebuilt according to a project by Laurynas Stuoka-Gucevičius in a strict Classical style (his design included a tower with a statue of King Stanislaus August, but it was never constructed). In the new building there were rooms for guards, a prison, nine shops; weapons, standard metres and measures were kept there; the building housed halls of the governor and the mer-

The main façade of the Town Hall

Interior of the
Town Hall

chants' association and treasuries of the city and the merchants' association.

The great hall was famous for its acoustics. During the tsarist occupation concerts used to be held there. In 1810 the entire building was converted into a theatre – first Polish, later Russian. In 1854 the premiere of Stanisław Moniuszko's opera *Halka* took place in the Town Hall; the composer himself conducted the orchestra. In 1906 a Lithuanian tragedy *Duke of Pilėnai* by Marcelinas Šikšnys was performed in the theatre. In 1918–19 "The Flying Theatre" of Juozas Vaičkus gave performances in the Town Hall. In 1936–40 the building was renovated. In 1941 an art museum was established there. Now the building houses the Artists' Palace.

Contemporary Art
Centre (Vokiečių St. 2)

The most beautiful part of the Town Hall is a forceful simple portico of six Doric columns with a triangular pediment. The Great Hall and other halls have survived, as well as the Gothic and later vaults, in which the magistrate's chest and other objects related

Radisson SAS Astorija Hotel (Didžioji St. 35/2)

with the history of the Town Hall are presently on display. On the south side of the building there is an entry to "Freskos" café, whose décor is reminiscent of the history of the Vilnius theatre. The surviving frescoes date from Stuoka-Gucevičius' times.

Close to the Town Hall, at Vokiečių St. 2, stands a newer palace of the Contemporary Art Centre that harmonizes rather well with the old town buildings (architect Vytautas Čekanauskas, 1965–67).

## Abramavičienė estate

The building south of the Church of St. Casimir (Didžioji St. 36) was traditionally misnamed the Brzostowski estate. Having

Abramavičienė estate (Didžioji St. 36)

acquired several houses on this site in 1790, M. Abramavičienė had them reconstructed into a three-storey symmetrical early Classical building (architect Martin Knackfuss). Later both the proprietors, as well as the appearance of the building, changed. Now it houses the Conservatoire. On the opposite side of the street stands one of the oldest Vilnius hotels "Astorija" (called "Italia" before the Second World War). It has been renovated according to world standards.

## Aušros Vartų Street

This street ends in the only surviving gate of the defensive wall – Medininkų, or Aušros Gate. As if symbolizing the diversity of Vilnius religions, it is a meeting place of three sanctuaries of different confessions: the Uniate Church of the Holy Trinity, the Russian Orthodox Church and Monastery of the Holy Trinity, the

Aušros Vartų St. 8

Catholic Church of St. Theresa, and the Monastery of the Barefoot Carmelites with the Aušros Vartų Chapel. From the façade of St. Theresa's the street turns into a kind of open-air church, where according to Vilnius tradition a cap should not be worn.

The street boasts many interesting buildings. Among them No. 8, a building with sgraffiti trimmings, should be distinguished. It is the only building in Vilnius that served an auxiliary function in the 15th–16th cent. (apparently a warehouse). Its history goes back to the 15th cent. or early 16th cent., the façades were decorated in sgraffiti (black and white ornaments) in the late 16th cent. In 1970–74 the house was renovated. On the other side of the street (No. 13) stands a house with typical three-storey wooden galleries in the courtyard.

The main façade of the Philharmonic Society

## Philharmonic Society ㉗

It is a former palace of the City Hall built in 1902 (architect Konstantin Koroyedov). Until the early 20th cent. a Gothic inn of Russian merchants stood on this site (1501). The Philharmonic Society (Aušros Vartų St. 5) is one of the most magnificent Historicist buildings in Vilnius. From 1904 it housed a Lithuanian bookshop, and on December 4–5th 1905 the Great Seimas of Vilnius that demanded autonomy for Lithuania took place in this building. On November 6th 1906 the first Lithuanian opera *Birutė* by Mikas Petrauskas was presented there. In the times of Soviet occupation there was a tendency to emphasize the fact that on December 15th 1918 local communists and other leftist parties proclaimed a short-lived Soviet Lithuanian Republic in the City Hall. Later the palace housed an assembly hall, theatre and cinema hall, and in 1940 the Philharmonic Society was established there. Fedor Shalyapin, and after 1945 many world-famous soloists and ensembles performed on tour in this hall.

Gate of the Basilian
Monastery from Aušros
Vartų Street

Gate and belfry of the
Basilian Monastery
from the courtyard

## Church of the Holy Trinity
## and the Basilian Monastery 28

Further up the street from the Philharmonic Society stands a particularly elegant rolling gate of the Basilian Monastery (Aušros
Vartų St. 7b) – one of the most beautiful late Baroque monuments
in Vilnius (architect Jan Krzysztof Glaubitz, 1761). It is decorated
with a composition glorifying the Holy Trinity. Entering through
an arch, one gets into a spacious courtyard, in the middle of which
stands a cube-shaped church with elements of the Gothic, Baroque
and Russian Byzantine style. A monastery is located on the Hill of
the Holy Trinity famous as the place where in pagan times three
Lithuanian Christian martyrs Anthony, John and Eustatius were
killed. According to a legend, Juliana, the wife of Algirdas, built a
wooden church in their memory in 1347. The church that survived
into our days was built with funding by Constantine Ostrogsky in
1514 as a Russian Orthodox church. In 1608–1827 the church and
the monastery belonged to the Uniate Basilian monks. Later it was
passed on to the Russian Orthodox believers, and recently went
back to the Uniates. Massive apses, open-worked late Baroque
towers on the eastern façade and an isolated belfry of archaic
appearance (16th cent.) should be mentioned in particular. A late
16th cent. relief tombstone plaque in memory of Vilnius burgomaster Anastazy Braha and his son Anthony with an inscription in
Cyrillic characters is set up inside.

Apse of the Church of
the Holy Trinity

Courtyard of the
Basilian Monastery,
farther – entrance to
the Conrad cell

The monastery buildings were built together with the church and later were reconstructed several times (a round tower in the north-west was added in the 2nd half of the 19th cent.). It housed a Russian Orthodox printing house that published the first Eastern Slavonic ABC book by Lavrentii Zizanius in 1596, as well as some Lithuanian books. In the early 19th cent. a prison was established in the south building of the monastery. In 1823–24, participants of the Philaret and Philomat case, among them Adam Mickiewicz and Ignacy Domejko (who later emigrated to South America and became the first minister of education in Chile), were imprisoned there. Having bribed the guards, prisoners used to gather in a quite spacious cell of Mickiewicz at night. This cell received the name of Conrad, since in it the character of Mickiewicz's drama *The Fore-fathers' Eve* named Conrad experienced an inner struggle with God and Satan, a spiritual revival and pronounced the Great Impro-visation – one of the most remarkable monologues in the history of world literature. The location of the Conrad cell was established by Juliusz Kłos in the 1920's. A memorial plaque with a Latin text from *The Forefathers' Eve*: *DOM Gustavus. Obiit MDCCCXXIII cal-endis Novembris. Hic natus est Conradus MDCCCXXIII calendis Novembris* (On November 1st 1823 Gustav died here; on November 1st 1823 Conrad was born here) is set into the wall of the cell. Literary events are held there.

Members of the 1830–31 uprising, as well as the revolutionary Szymon Konarski (executed in 1839), were imprisoned in the mo-nastery. In the 1st half of the 20th cent. a Byelorussian high school, a scientific society and a museum operated there. A small part of the former monastery is now occupied by Basilian monks, and some of the premises are used by the Gediminas Technical University

## Russian Orthodox Church of the Holy Spirit and the monastery ensemble ㉙

A Russian Orthodox church and monastery (Aušros Vartų St. 10) have been operating on this site since 1567. A wooden church was

Russian Orthodox
Church of the Holy Spirit

Iconostasis of the Russian
Orthodox Church of
the Holy Spirit

built in 1638; it was reconstructed and decorated in the rococo style by Jan Krzysztof Glaubitz in 1749–53. The church is interesting as an example of Vilnius Baroque, being the only Russian Orthodox sanctuary of this type in Lithuania. Its serene symmetrical appearance with twin early Baroque towers and a high (49 m) cupola is supplemented by a plain massive belfry. The interior is noted for an abundant 18th cent. décor: a typical wooden iconostasis (apparently designed by Glaubitz in 1756–57) is reminiscent of a Catholic altar. The plan of the church is also Catholic-style, in the form of a Latin cross. The church holds 12 paintings by Ivan Trutnev (19th cent.). In 1826–51 an underground crypt with the remains of the Orthodox saints John, Eustatius and Anthony was erected. In 1852 the remains of the three holy martyrs were moved to a new reliquary, where they rest now. On June 26th of each year the Russian Orthodox believers celebrate the day of moving these relics. During a special service the reliquary is unveiled – the relics are thought to have a healing power. The church acquired its present appearance after a reconstruction in 1873 initiated by Muravyov: the cupola was rebuilt, and the façade was transformed by pulling down volutes and a curving pediment between the towers. A late Baroque belfry was rebuilt in the Classical style.

A monastery building (closer to the street) was built in the late 15th or early 16th cent. and renovated in 1821–25. A late 16th cent. convent building (right of the church) was reconstructed in 1842–44. Both buildings have Gothic elements.

The Monastery of the Holy Spirit nurtured outstanding Russian Orthodox intellectuals: Meletii Smotrycki who compiled the first *Slavic Grammar* (Vievis, 1619), archimandrite Piotr Mohyla, who published a Russian Orthodox prayer book in Kiev in 1646. The monastery funded the Vievis printing house. At a monastery school Russian, Polish, Latin and Greek, as well as logic and dialectics were taught. At the present time 12 monks live in the monastery; it is the only Russian Orthodox monastery operating in Lithuania.

## Church of St. Theresa and the Monastery of the Barefoot Carmelites ㉚

Church of St. Theresa and Aušros Gate

Memorial plaque on the wall of the Pociej Chapel

One of the most excellent early Baroque monuments in Vilnius. The church (Aušros Vartų St. 14) was built in 1633–50 under the patronage of the Vice Chancellor of the Grand Duchy Stephen Pac (it is thought that the architect was Ulrich, and the façade was designed by Constantino Tencalla). Expensive materials, such as Swedish sandstone, granite and marble, were used for construction. The monastery dates from 1621–27, and was built with funding by the Vilnius burgomaster Ignacy Dubowicz and his brother Stefan. In 1763–65 the church interior was decorated with sculptures and frescoes, partly destroyed by Napoleon's soldiers in 1812; in 1783 m. the Pociej Chapel – a mausoleum of the noblemen's family – was added. The church was renovated after 1812, in 1927–29 and 1971–76.

The façade of the Church of St. Theresa was designed according to the models of Roman architecture: it is noble and harmonious, built along the vertical principle, and accentuated by volutes and side obelisks. A massive octagonal belfry is crowned with a weathervane – an angel with a trumpet. The interior looks quite different, it is in the rococo style (with the exception of the Pociej Chapel, which is late Baroque on the exterior, and rather Classical in the interior). The church is built along a basilican design and has a wide central and two narrow side naves and a blind cupola (unseen from the outside). In this space of moderate proportions,

an astounding view of fantastically rich picturesque décor unfolds: the high altar is made of sandstone with a profiled cornice, a relief pediment in the shape of clouds, curious pilasters-volutes and numerous sculptures, – it is one of the most beautiful in Lithuania. Mural paintings, dating from the 2nd half of the 18th cent. (artist Maciej Słuszczański), were renovated in 1927–29. Scenes representing the life of St. Theresa decorate the vaults and walls of the central nave; the vaults of the side chapels have painted emblems – all of them form a harmonious whole. The pulpit, confessionals and pews are in the rococo style. Paintings by Szymon Czechowicz, Kanuty Rusiecki and other artists are to be found in the church.

Interior of the Church of St. Theresa

The early Baroque monastery buildings are moderate and simple; picturesque courtyards are divided by arches. The Barefoot Carmelites of Vilnius used to brew beer famous in the whole city, and mould candles. The monastery gave funding to secular students of medicine and took care of old people and orphans.

## Aušros Gate ㉛

Aušros Gate

It is one of the symbols of Vilnius – a Catholic sanctuary famous in all Lithuania and even abroad, respected by other confessions as well.

A gate built on the road to Medininkai, Ašmena and Minsk, initially called Medininkų Gate, was one of the first five Vilnius gates erected together with the city wall (1503–22). They were first mentioned in historical sources in 1514. The name "Aušros Gate" is

Aušros Gate from the
south

1. Basilian Church and
monastery
2. Russian Orthodox
Church of the Holy
Spirit and monastery
3. Church of St. Theresa
and the Carmelite
Monastery
4. Aušros (Medininkų)
Gate

probably derived from "Aštrieji Gate", as the gate was located in
the southern side of the city called Aštrusis (Sharp); gradually
because of the cult of Virgin Mary it was associated with sunrise.
The gate has a square plan and Gothic masonry (except for a
Renaissance top and attic), the wall is 2–2.6 m thick. The entry arch
is covered by a cylindrical vault. There are some traces of a heavy
iron gate under the arch. Loopholes can be seen on the south side;
among them is a niche with a cross, above it – a cornice with a
sculptural head of the patron of merchants (and thieves) Hermes,
or Mercury. Higher up is a Renaissance attic with architectural
motifs and two relief-work griffins, holding the Lithuanian coat-of-
arms Vytis. On the east (right) side of the gate stretches a sizeable
section of the city wall (the largest of all surviving sections).

The painting of the Mother of Mercy of Aušros Gate is known to all
Catholics of the world. Many copies of this painting are found in
churches of various countries, even, e.g., in the Church of St. Seve-
rin in Paris, and in the Basilica of St. Peter in Rome, a Chapel of
Aušros Gate has been appointed. The painting of the Holy Virgin
Mary, called the Madonna of Vilnius, is dated by the 1st quarter of
the 17th cent. It is painted in the Renaissance style. The Virgin
Mary is depicted without Child, with her head tilted to the right,
her hands are crossed over her chest, her eyes are half-closed, with
a soft and graceful silhouette. The painting was executed with tempera on oak planks and later painted over in oil paint. Since the
middle of the 17th cent. it is considered miraculous. In 1688 the
painting was entrusted to the care of the Carmelite monks who

Votive objects in the
Chapel of Aušros Gate

Mother of Mercy in the
Chapel of Aušros Gate

Relief work on the attic
of Aušros Gate with
the Vytis sign

lived at the Church of St. Theresa. Atop the gate they built a wooden, and later brick, Baroque chapel, into which the painting from the church was transferred. In the 1st third of the 18th cent. a sumptuous framing for the painting from gilded silver with wrought roses, tulips, narcissi and carnations, was finished, most probably by the Vilnius goldsmiths' guild. There is a large silver half-moon at the bottom of the painting. In the 20th cent. the painting was twice adorned with crowns sent by the Pope, thus conferring the Mother of God of Aušros Gate the title of Mother of Mercy. In 1993, before the Pope's visit, the painting and the framing was renovated. In 1829 the reconstructed chapel acquired some features of Classicism. It is decorated with pilasters of the Doric order, a relief work of the Eye of Providence on the tympanum and a Latin inscription: *Mater Misericordiae, sub Tuum Praesidium confugimus* (Mother of Mercy, we pray for your protection).

A stone staircase, built in 1799 on the right to St. Theresa's, leads to a pilgrim gallery at the painting. Almost 8,000 silver votive objects are hung in the chapel. During his visit in Vilnius (1993), Pope John Paul II prayed there and showed a special honour to Mary of Aušros Gate. Adam Mickiewicz, Juliusz Słowacki, Władysław Syrokomla wrote poems dedicated to the Madonna of Vilnius. Stanisław Moniuszko composed four litanies to Aušros Gate. In 1914, the famous Russian poet Anna Akhmatova prayed at Aušros Gate, seeing off her husband Nikolai Gumilev, who was going to the war.

# Vilnius ghetto

A mediaeval Vilnius Jewish ghetto was located west of Didžioji St. and stretched up to Dominikonų and Vokiečių streets; somewhat later it expanded to the other side of Vokiečių St. towards Pylimo St.

In the 19th – early 20th cent. Jews lived in other city areas as well. At the beginning of the Second World War the Vilnius Jewish population counted 55–60 thousand people. On September 6–7th these who did not manage to escape and were not killed in the first days of the war, were driven into two ghettoes separated by Vokiečių St. In the small ghetto (Stiklių, Gaono, Antokolskio, Žydų St.) lived 11–12 thousand Jews, mainly intellectuals, blue collar workers and disabled people; the large, or craftsmen, ghetto (Rūdninkų, Mėsinių, Ašmenos, Žemaitijos, Dysnos, Šiaulių, Ligoninės St.) counted 29 thousand people. All of them suffered severe discrimination, hunger and dire living conditions; the majority were subjected to forced labour, and in the autumn of 1941 the annihilation of the Vilnius Jews began. The ghettoes were isolated from the city, house windows along the borders of ghettoes were painted over and boarded up. The small ghetto survived until October 21st 1941, and the large ghetto was liquidated by the Nazis on August 23rd 1943. After August, in the course of liquidating the ghetto, physically fit persons were sent to work camps in Latvia and Estonia, and the disabled – to the Maidanek death camp. 2–3 thousand Jews were left in work camps in Vilnius.

Žydų Street. 1937.
Photo by Jan Bułhak

Plan of the ghetto

1. Great Synagogue
2. Strashun Library
3. Ramailes Lane
4. Gaon's Synagogue
5. Synagogue of the Funeral Fraternity
6. The Old and the New (Yesod) Synagogue
7. Mitzvah (ritual bath)
8. A well

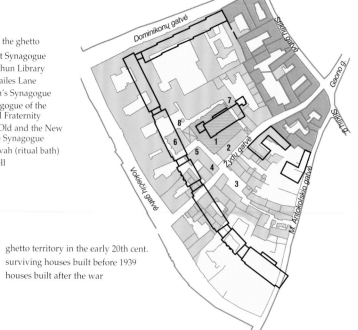

ghetto territory in the early 20th cent.

surviving houses built before 1939

houses built after the war

The Great Synagogue.
1910's.
Photo by Jan Bułhak

Aron Ha Kodesh of the
Great Synagogue. 1930.
Photo by Jan Bułhak

During the period of Soviet occupation the ruins of the ghettoes turned into desolate places, and their history was passed over in silence.

Some fragments of early architecture either have survived or have been restored in the small ghetto, first of all – houses on Stiklių St. (No. 6, 8, 12) and Gaono St. (No. 6, 7/11). On Žydų St. stood the Great Synagogue that could accommodate 3–5 thousand believers; 18 Torah scrolls were held there. Nearby stood the Gaon prayer house, the famous Strashun Library, more than ten synagogues and other buildings of religious purpose. After the war all of them were finally destroyed by Soviet authorities. A kindergarten was built on the site of the Great Synagogue, next to it a monument to the Gaon has been erected (a house where he lived stood on that site).

The main gate of the large ghetto was situated on Rūdninkų St. (No. 18). The former Ogiński estate at Rūdninkų St. 8 was a meeting place of the Ghetto Council (Judenrat) led by an officer of the Lithuanian army Jacob Gens, killed by the Gestapo on September 14th 1943. At Ašmenos St. 8 and Žemaitijos (Strašuno) St. 4, Jewish guerilla centres were functioning. In the present "Lėlė" Theatre a ghetto theatre operated after 1942. In 1988 this theatre presented a performance after the famous drama *Ghetto* by Joshua Sobol, dedicated to the history of the ghetto theatre. In 1997 the 55th anniversary of the theatre was celebrated.

To commemorate the 50th anniversary of the liquidation of the ghetto, memorial stones for martyrs and fighters of the ghetto, and for the old Jewish cemetery destroyed in 1950 were set up in the centre of Vilnius in 1993. A square in the territory of the former ghetto is called the Square of Ghetto Victims.

Vokiečių Street

## Vokiečių Street ㉜

It is one of the oldest streets in Vilnius, mentioned since 1576. Before the Second World War Vokiečių St. was a commercial centre. Large shops were most often situated on the first floor, and small ones – in courtyards and gateways. In the post-war period, Soviet architects obsessed with megalomania took advantage of the fact that houses on the east side of the street were partly destroyed, and decided to lay a road that was supposed to intersect the old town up to Žaliasis Bridge. The street was widened four times, and a "tape-worm" house was build lengthwise. Monuments of architecture that could have been renovated were destroyed. Old buildings survived only on the west side.

Detail of Vokiečių St. 20

Vokiečių St. 18/12, 20

No. 18/12, 20 – a complex that includes the Evangelical Lutheran Church and associated houses. The first Evangelical church (Kirche) was built on this site in 1555 on the initiative of the Chancellor of the Grand Duchy Nicholas Radziwiłł the Black. The surrounding houses were occupied mainly by Evangelical Lutherans. The church was rebuilt in 1662 and substantially reconstructed in 1738–44. In 1944 it was closed down. In 1993 it was returned to its parishioners and renovated. The church has a single nave and an original pentagonal shape; its magnificent high altar was designed by architect Jan Krzysztof Glaubitz. The height of the belfry is 30 m, the top part was built in 1872. Atop the tower sits a high tin-plated spire with a weathervane containing an inscription "1555–1955".

Tyzenhaus, or Wittinghoff estate (No. 28/17)

Evangelical Lutheran Church

No. 22 – Worbeck-Lettow's house. Known since the 16th cent. In the 17th cent. Christopher Radziwiłł gave it to the king's doctor Matthew Worbeck-Lettow. Later it belonged to the Evangelical Lutheran community that had established an almshouse there. It has some elements of Gothic and Baroque.

No. 24 – Hozius' house. It was built by the Vilnius castle keeper and administrator of the mint Ulrich Hozius in the 1st half of the 16th cent. The house has some features of Gothic and Renaissance, and particularly interesting Gothic vaults, presently occupied by the pub "Žemaičių smuklė".

No. 26. In this house the famous Polish composer Stanisław Moniuszko lived in 1840–58.

No. 28/17 – Tyzenhaus, or Wittinghoff estate. A building on this site is mentioned since 1597. In the 2nd half of the 18th cent. it was basically reconstructed and expanded by the Vice Treasurer of Lithuania Antanas Tyzenhauzas (Antoni Tyzenhaus). After his bankruptcy and death, the building was reconstructed again in 1790 and acquired its present appearance, its monumental Classical façades remained unchanged until our times. It is one of the most superb works by a popular period architect Martin Knackfuss. The Silver Hall on the first floor was widely famous. Damaged during the Second World War, the building was renovated in 1957.

Hozius' house (No. 24)

Radziwiłł Palace
(No. 41/9)

## Vilniaus Street

One of the major axes of the city (formerly called Vilijos St.). It is a
continuation of Vokiečių St. leading to Gedimino Ave. and farther
up to Žaliasis Bridge.

No. 39/6 (in front of a square with a monument to Moniuszko).
Built in the late 19th cent.; in 1904–06 the first Lithuanian daily
*Vilniaus žinios* (Vilnius News) edited by Petras Vileišis was
published there. Presently it accommodates the Vilnius Teachers'
House.

Vilniaus St. 39/6

No. 41/9 – Radziwiłł Palace. In the late 16th cent. three houses,
connected into one building in the 17th cent., stood on this site. The
Palace has both Renaissance and Baroque features. In 1796–1810
Vilnius City Theatre operated there. When it was moved to the
Town Hall, various theatre companies used to perform there until
1845. Premises of the former theatre are located on the southeast
part of the Palace (their plan has survived). Presently it houses the
Museum of Theatre, Music and Cinema.

## Church of St. Catherine
## and the Benedictine Convent ㉝

The Church of St. Catherine (Vilniaus St. 30) is regarded by art historians as the most typical example of Vilnius Baroque. This type
of late Baroque churches is noted for slender and elegant twin towers. A picturesque silhouette of the Church of St. Catherine stands
out in the whole panorama of the old town.

The history of the ensemble goes back to 1618, when hetman John
Carol Chodkiewicz and his wife Sophia invited Benedictine nuns
from Nesvizh to Vilnius. They built for them a small brick church,
which was later expanded and after the 1741–73 reconstruction
(architect Jan Krzysztof Glaubitz) acquired its present appearance.
The church was damaged in 1812 and during the Second World
War, but was restored afterwards.

The church façade is dominated by vertical lines. It is abundantly
decorated, the pediment and towers are adorned with volutes,
vases and beautiful open-worked crosses with rays. Above the
pediment hangs the Chodkiewicz coat-of-arms. The back pediment with numerous relief works is also impressive. Flanking it on
Vilniaus St. a particularly elegant Chapel of Providence was erected (1641, rebuilt in 1746). This single-nave church has 9 magnifi-

Church of St. Catherine

cent late Baroque altars and a pulpit. Presently the church is under renovation.

Convent buildings date from the 16th–19th cent. Noteworthy is the great courtyard with arch windows of the cloister, and a Baroque portal in the northwest courtyard. The buildings are distinguished by their complex plan. The 17th–18th cent. was a period when the convent thrived. Sybill and Anne, daughters of the Vice-Governor of the Grand Duchy John Felix Pac, became nuns of this convent and brought along a large dowry. The convent funded book publishing and accumulated a library that was one of the largest in the congregation (it is presently held at the National M. Mažvydas Library). Having endured a period of hardship in the 19th cent., the convent recovered in the early 20th cent.: thanks to the efforts of abbess Julia Anzelma Miliczówna it regained some of its lands and established a high school.

In front of the church, a bust of composer Stanisław Moniuszko (sculptor Bolesław Bałzukiewicz) stands in a small square. It was built in 1922; the pedestal was taken from a monument to Pushkin which stood at the foot of the Gediminas Hill since 1899 (during the First World War Pushkin's bust was moved to Russia). On the other side of the church, close to the apse, stands a monument to poetess Salomėja Nėris (sculptor Vladas Vildžiūnas, 1973).

Monument to Stanisław Moniuszko

Tyszkiewicz Estate
(Trakų St. 1/26)

Statue of "The City
Guard" in the niche
of the Umiastowski
estate (Trakų St. 2)

Church of Evangelical
Reformers

## Tyszkiewicz Estate and the Church of Evangelical Reformers ㉞ ㉟

The Tyszkiewicz estate is located at Trakų St. 1/26. To the west of the palace runs Pylimo St., while Kėdainių St., a typical Vilnius lane, lies eastwards. This is one of the most significant Empire style buildings in Vilnius. In 1783 a house on this site, mentioned since the 15th cent., was reconstructed by Laurynas Stuoka-Gucevičius, and in 1840 – by Tomasz Tyszecki. In the middle of the 19th cent. Nikolaj Chagin added a portal with statues of the Atlantes (sculptors Franciszek Andriolli and Józef Kozłowski). In this palace Eustachy Tyszkiewicz held part of his archaeological collections that constituted the basis of the Museum of Antiquities. In 1863 it was a secret gathering place of the rebels. Later it housed the offices of the Jewish community. The building is adorned by the Tyszkiewicz coat-of-arms on the pediment, high-relief male and female heads, and the interior boasts an abundant Classical décor. At the present time the building is occupied by the Vilnius Gediminas Technical University.

In front of it, at Trakų St. 2, stands the Umiastowski estate. It is a monument of late Classicism (the 2nd half of the 18th cent., the façades date from the early 20th cent.) On this site stood the Trakų Gate of the city defensive wall (a section of the wall can be seen from the courtyard). There is a niche looking at Pylimo St. It once held a statue of the patron of Vilnius, St. Christopher, destroyed after the Second World War. In 1973 a statue of "The City Guard" was erected in the niche (sculptor Stanislovas Kuzma).

In the north (Pylimo St. 18) stands the Church of Evangelical Reformers (Calvinists), designed in a strict Classical style by Karol Pod-

Detail of the ceiling of the Church of Evangelical Reformers

czaszyński in 1830–35. Its pediment is decorated by a high-relief work "Christ Speaking for the Crowds" (sculptor Kazimierz Jelski). There is a valuable coffer ceiling with floral ornaments in the interior. The main façade has an elegantly proportioned portico of six Corinthian columns. Atop the pediment stood three sculptures by Kazimierz Jelski that did not survive. In the Soviet period the building housed a cinema theatre. Recently it has been returned to its parishioners.

The belfry of the Franciscan Church. Before 1867. Photo by Józef Czechowicz

## Church of the Assumption of the Holy Virgin Mary and the Franciscan Monastery ㊱

The ensemble is situated in between Trakų, Kėdainių, Lydos and Pranciškonų streets. It is a very archaic area in Vilnius. The Franciscans established themselves on this site before Lithuania's Christianization. Their church is one of the oldest city buildings: a brick church or chapel stood on this site as early as the middle of the 14th cent. Burial sites dating from the late 13th – early 14th cent. have been discovered. They were party destroyed while laying the church foundations. Thus, before the construction of a brick church, a cemetery was located on this site, apparently at a wooden

Franciscan Church

Gothic tower of the
Franciscan Church

Monument to Józef
Montwiłł

church. Burials took place according to Christian traditions. This
allows us to assume that it is one of the earliest Catholic sites in
Vilnius.

The church (Trakų St. 9/1) is Gothic, with some Baroque forms that
it acquired in the late 18th cent. In 1812 the church was partly
destroyed by the French army that used it as a granary; in 1864
Muravyov closed it down and converted it into an archive. In the
1930's the church was returned to the Franciscan monks. In the
Soviet times it again held an archive; recently it was returned to its
parishioners and renovation works began.

The general proportions of the church, a pointed arch of the portal,
and a round tower north of the façade bear witness to the early
Gothic period. Impressive is the three-nave interior space (initially
it was hall-shaped) with two Gothic chapels on the south side at
the presbytery. In the chapels rib-and-panel vaults have survived.
On the north side there is one pre-Renaissance and one
Renaissance chapel, the latter dating from the early 17th cent.
Recently a statue of the Holy Virgin Mary (The White Mother of

God), considered miraculous, was returned to the church. South of the church stood an excellent Gothic quadrangular belfry with inlaid ornaments, pulled down in 1872.

The church adjoins a monastery, the oldest in Lithuania, whose construction began in Gediminas' times (1334). On its premises (at Lydos and Pranciškonų St.) the first two-grade Lithuanian school in Vilnius operated in 1908–24. In 1908–17 it housed the office of the Lithuanian Scholarly Society and for some time was home to Jonas Basanavičius.

At the crossing of Trakų and Pranciškonų streets stands a Baroque Suzin Chapel with an elegant portal and semi-round apses. Between the chapel and the church, a monument to Józef Montwiłł (Juozapas Montvila), a Vilnius burgomaster, public figure and patron, was erected in 1932 (sculptor Bolesław Bałzukiewicz). By his efforts a labour exchange of the society of aid for the poor was established in a desolate library hall of the monastery.

Suzin Chapel

## Church of St. Nicholas (37)

This church (Šv. Mikalojaus St. 4) is one of the oldest in Vilnius and Lithuania. Its Gothic features have survived almost unchanged. The church stood in the pagan Vilnius: it was first mentioned in 1387 (already at that time it was brick and had been built a long time ago). The Gothic pillars and vaults went up in the 16th cent. The belfry is Baroque, of moderate forms, and accords with the style of the church fairly well.

Interior of the Church of St. Nicholas

Church of St. Nicholas

Statue of St. Christopher

Detail of the façade

In 1901–39 the Church of St. Nicholas was the only church in Vilnius where the mass was held in Lithuanian. By the same token it was a centre of Lithuanian culture (its famous dean Kristupas Čibiras was killed in 1942 during a bombing raid). The church maintained the tradition of nurturing the Lithuanian national spirit in later times as well. During the Soviet occupation a statue of the patron of Vilnius, St. Christopher, was erected in the church orchard (sculptor Antanas Kmieliauskas, 1959); it was an obvious act of resistance, as the city's coat-of-arms with St. Christopher's figure was banned at that time.

Plain and even primitive, the redbrick building nevertheless attracts the eye by its coziness and tranquility. Its façade is flanked by two stocky buttresses with cut-off tops. Bricks are laid in the Gothic manner, in many places irregularly. The walls are not quite straight, the angles not quite right, and the apse has an irregular plan. Of the Gothic part, only the niches, edgings and pediments are plastered. The triangular pediment with niches has been recently renovated accentuating its original Gothic character. In the interior, four elegant octahedral pillars support web and star vaults. The high altar holds a painting of St. Nicholas with a silver setting from the 16th cent. The church is adorned with two sculptures: a polychrome statue of St. Louis from the Gothic period, and Vytautas' bronze bust erected in 1930 (sculptor Rapolas Jakimavičius).

## Synagogue ㊳

A choral synagogue (Pylimo St. 39) is the only one of 105 Vilnius synagogues and Judaic prayer houses that has survived. It was built in 1903 in the Moorish style. The façade contains an inscription in Hebrew: "A prayer house is sacred for all nations", and above the pediment the tablets with the Ten Commandments are represented. Today a small Jewish community of Vilnius gathers in the synagogue.

## Church of St. Stephen ㊴

The Church of St. Stephen (Geležinkelio St. 39) and the ensemble of the Monastery of St. Rochus, surrounded by industrial buildings, can be seen from a terrace of Geležinkelio St. This late Renaissance church (1600–12) is one of the earliest in Vilnius suburbs. St. Lazarus' almshouse operated at the church, plague and famine victims were buried there. In 1715 m. the church and the monastery were given to the brethren of St. Rochus who tended to sick people, and in 1752 – to the sisters of Mary. Severely damaged during a fire in 1794, the church was reconstructed and slightly transformed in 1801–06 (architect Pietro Rossi). The reconstruction works were accelerated by a gift of 3,000 silver roubles from tsar Paul I who was passing through Vilnius. In 1864 the convent was closed down,

Detail of the façade
of the synagogue

Church of St. Stephen

and the buildings converted into a prison; in 1926 it housed the stone-crushers' guild. In a cemetery at the church many outstanding people were buried, among others architect Laurynas Stuoka-Gucevičius (a memorial plaque to him is set up on the south façade of the church); later the cemetery was turned into a storage site of construction materials. In 1975–76 the façades were renovated, but the church is still in a shabby condition and does not function.

Church of All Saints

## Church of All Saints and its surroundings ④⓪

The church (Rūdninkų St. 20/1) was built in 1620–30 in the early Baroque (so-called Carmelite) style. A belfry was erected and the sculptures in the interior were created in the 18th cent. In 1859 the polychrome interior décor was enriched. In Soviet times the church housed a museum of folk art, and presently it has been returned to its parishioners.

Its steady and harmonious façade is somewhat reminiscent of the façade of the Church of St. Theresa. The high and massive belfry tower is magnificently decorated. There are 18 Baroque altars inside; above the high altar rises another altar reminiscent of a royal throne with a canopy (architect Martin Knackfuss).

A large old-regulation Carmelite monastery adjoins the church; it is built by adapting existing buildings. In 1631–32, the main two-storey building following the street was completed; there are also several buildings of a later period and a two-storey novitiate house with a small courtyard at the city wall. In the 16th–18th cent. they actively participated in public life, held religious feasts and processions. In 1819 the Carmelites established a parochial school in the monastery.

Karmelitų St. 3

East of the church lies a square, in which the Convent of the Barefoot Carmelites once stood alongside a Baroque Church of St. Joseph the Betrothed established in 1638 by the Vice-Chancellor of the Grand Duchy Stephen Pac. Its exterior was reminiscent of the Church of St. Theresa. In 1877 the Church of St. Joseph the Betrothed was demolished by the tsar's order, to be replaced by a market, popularly called Basokai (presently it is a square).

At Rūdninkų St. 10, north of the Church of All Saints, is a house that belonged to the citizen Frez and his descendants in the 17th cent. Its appearance is typical of the period – Baroque, with some Renaissance elements. During the Second World War the house stood in the territory of the ghetto. It was renovated in 1977–80.

On Arklių St. (No. 5) stands the Ogiński estate – a stately 18th cent. early Classical building with large courtyards. It houses the Youth and the "Lėlė" Theatres. There are more houses-monuments in the vicinity: Arklių St. 4 (Gothic), Karmelitų St. 3 (with renovated Gothic details on the exterior and 17th cent. decorative roofbeams in the interior), Karmelitų St. 4 (Classical, with Gothic vaults).

Church of St. Joseph the Betrothed. Ca. 1872–74. Photo by Józef Czechowicz

Arklių St. 4

Rūdninkų St. 10

Bastion of the city wall

# Bastion ㊶ ㊷

East of Aušros Vartų St., in front of the Philharmonic Society, starts Subačiaus St. It leads to a place where the Subačiaus Gate, the strongest gate of the city wall, once stood. Two sections of the wall with loopholes have survived: ca. 30 m at the crossing of Subačiaus and Strazdelio streets, and ca. 150 m on Bokšto St. towards the hillside. At Bokšto St. 20/18 the Bastion (Barbican) is located. It consists of an original tower of the city wall, a hemispherical canon room and a corridor connecting it with the tower. The Gediminas Hill and the Vilnia valley offer a good view of the whole complex of the Bastion. It was apparently designed by the military engineer Friedrich Getkant in the 1st half of the 17th cent. Partly destroyed during the 1655–61 war with Moscow, the Bastion was later turned into a dump. During the First and Second World War it was used as a hideout and a depot. The vaults of the Bastion are associated with a legend about the basilisk of Vilnius – a dragon whose look used to turn people into stone; the basilisk itself turned into stone on seeing its mirror reflection. Before the Second World War students' carnival processions with an image of the basilisk were popular.

The walls and moats of the Bastion were excavated in 1965–70, and the canon room was renovated in 1985–86. The entire Bastion was converted into a museum, and since 1987 it houses an exhibition of defensive fortifications and weaponry.

Strazdelio St. branches off south of Subačiaus St. In 1900–40, the Romm printing house, at that time the largest Jewish printing house in the world, was situated at No. 1.

Former Romm
printing house
from Strazdelio St.

## Bokšto Street

City wall on Bokšto St.
End of the 19th cent.
Photo by
Stanisław Fleury

It is thought that a settlement existed on this site before Gediminas' and even Mindaugas' times, in the 12th cent. There are several interesting buildings on this street.

No. 2 – in the 19th cent. it housed a hotel. For some time one of the leaders of the 1863 uprising Zigmunt Sierakowski lived there. Anticipating the uprising, a military council took place in this house.

No. 6 – Savičius hospital. In the 16th cent. a Gothic house that was acquired by the Savičius (Sawicz) family in the 18th cent., stood on this site. In 1747, the colonel of the Nowogródek district Juozapas Savičius Korsakas (Józef Sawicz Korsak) donated the house to medical nurses. It was connected with other buildings and converted into a hospital. From 1803 medical students under Professor Józef Frank worked there, and in 1831–32 it housed university clinics. The hospital continued operating both in the inter-war and Soviet period. The building has some Baroque features; particularly interesting is its Baroque gate.

Gate of the Sawicz
Hospital (Bokšto St. 6)

No. 8 – in this house Józef Piłsudski (1867–1935), the restorer of Poland's independence and a state leader descending from Lithuanian noblemen spent his childhood and early youth. The Poles regard him as one of the most remarkable national heroes, while the Lithuanians take a more moderate attitude, since it was by his order that Vilnius was torn away from Lithuania and annexed by Poland in 1920.

Bokšto St. 2

No. 10 – Roemers' house. Its history goes back to the 16th cent. From the 18th cent. it belonged to the Roemer family that moved here from Livonia. Among the members of that family were several famous artists who had studios here; the house was called the Roemer Academy. Painters Kanuty and Bolesław Rusiecki, and Jan Zenkiewicz worked in the house; it was home to the compiler of the famous *Album de Wilna* Jan Kazimierz Wilczyński, and a place where Stanisław Moniuszko gave concerts. From 1781 a mason lodge "The Zealous Lithuanian" operated there. In 1977 the house was renovated.

Missionary Church

Vestibule of the
Missionary Church

## Church of the Assumption
## and the Missionary Monastery ㊸

The construction of the ensemble of the Missionary Church of the
Assumption (Subačiaus St. 28) and the Missionary Monastery
began in 1695 behind the former city wall, at Subačiaus Gate, on
the so-called Saviour Hill (a church is also often called by this
name). In 1750–56 it was basically reconstructed by architect Jan
Krzysztof Glaubitz. The church is one of the most subtle and
elegant late Baroque buildings in Vilnius. Its light and well-
proportioned towers with rounded corners adorned with decorative vases, lattices and open-worked crosses, attract the view from
afar. The front and back pediments are dynamic and have rolling
forms. The vestibule is a picturesque domical rotunda: it is echoed
by the pediment of the servants' house on the left. In the interior,
an altar to St. Vincent de Paul (also late Baroque) should be mentioned; frescoes from the 18th cent. have survived. In 1844 the
church and the monastery was closed down by the tsar's order.

From 1862 on services were held in the church again. In the Soviet period the church was closed down, and in 1993 returned to its parishioners.

The Missionary (St. Paul) Monastery is adjacent to the church; its eastern part is the former Sanguszko estate built in 1640–50. In 1773–1844, the ecclesiastical seminary of the Vilnius bishopric operated in the building. The seminary was famous for its library (considered the largest among Vilnius monasteries). Since 1803 a parish school operated there; later it was a place of imprisonment for several participants of the 1830–31 uprising. The function of the monastery changed more than once: it was used as a war hospital (1844), a Russian Orthodox consistory (1848), an Institute of Noble Girls (1856), a psychiatric hospital (1859), a welfare society (1874) etc. Presently it houses a hospital.

## Church of the Heart of Jesus
## and the Convent of the Visitationists ㊹

The Church of the Heart of Jesus, or the Visitationists Church (Rasų St. 6) and the Convent of the Visitationists is situated close to the Missionary Church, and together they constitute an impressive ensemble on the Saviour Hill that can be seen well from different sites of the city. The Visitationist nuns arrived in Vilnius in 1694 (invited by Bishop Constantine Brzostowski); a convent (endowed by Anna Dezelsztowa) was built for them in 1694–1797. Since its founding to 1843 the nuns maintained a boarding school that accommodated ca. 40 girls each year.

Visitationists Church

The church is a significant monument of early Baroque (apparently finished in 1756; architect Joseph Pola). It is the only Catholic church in Lithuania built along a Greek cross design. The church has a large octagonal cupola and a very rich elegant façade. The interior is no less magnificent, though severely damaged during the Soviet occupation. The altars of the church once held paintings by Szymon Czechowicz that are now part of the collections of the Lithuanian Art Museum. After the Second World War a prison was established in the buildings. The church interior and the plan of the convent buildings have been transformed.

Rasų Cemetery

Tombstone for
M.K. Čiurlionis

Tombstone for
Ludwik Kondratowicz-
Władysław Syrokomla

Grave of the mother
of Józef Piłsudski,
Maria, with the heart
of Piłsudski

## Rasų Cemetery ㊺

It is probably the most remarkable cemetery in Vilnius established
in 1800 by the dean of the Missionary Church of the Assumption
Tymoteusz Raczyński, who received from the magistrate a plot of
land of 3.51 ha behind the Church of the Visitationists. Later the
cemetery was expanded several times. In 1841 a neo-Gothic chapel
was erected in its centre. Today burials no longer take place in the
Rasų Cemetery, its role as a pantheon of Lithuania was taken over
by the Antakalnio Cemetery. During the Soviet occupation the cemetery was a place of patriotic manifestations of both Lithuanians
and Poles (particularly on All Souls' Day).

In the central area of the Rasų Cemetery lie many famous Lithuanian, Polish and Belorussian cultural figures. Numerous exquisite
tombstones of high artistic value can be found there. To the left of
the entry, on the so-called Literatų Hill, are the graves of Ludwik
Kondratowicz-Władysław Syrokomla, Gabrielius Landsbergis-Žemkalnis, Michał Roemer, Eustachy Tyszkiewicz, Petras Vaičiūnas,
Jan Kazimierz Wilczyński, Povilas Višinskis, Antanas Vivulskis
and others; the grave of Mikalojus Konstantinas Čiurlionis is situated on the highest part of the hill. Closer to the chapel or next to
it rest Jonas Basanavičius, Kazys Boruta, Mykolas Bukša, Petras
Cvirka, Kristupas Čibiras, Juliusz Kłos, Joachim Lelewel, Vincas
Mykolaitis-Putinas, Józef Montwiłł, Kipras and Mikas Petrauskas,
Karol Podczaszyński, Balys Sruoga, Marija and Jurgis Šlapelis,
Juozas Tallat-Kelpša, Juozas Tysliava and Petras Vileišis.

Lithuanian soldiers killed in 1920–21 in the battles for Vilnius, are
buried in another area of the cemetery (in the northwest corner of
the so-called Naujųjų Rasų Cemetery).

In a fenced-off area in front of the central gate, on the right, rest
Polish soldiers killed in 1919–20 and 1944. In the centre of this war
mausoleum, the mother of Józef Piłsudski, Maria, and the heart of

Piłsudski himself, lie under a black granite slab. The slab contains inscriptions from poems by Juliusz Słowacki. The grave was erected in 1936.

Library of the Academy of Sciences

## Library of the Academy of Sciences ㊻

By the Neris riverside (Žygimantų St. 1/8) stands the Library Palace built in 1885 on the site where the old Radziwiłł estate was once located, and where Barbora Radvilaitė (Barbara Radziwiłł) lived. The Library of the Lithuanian Academy of Sciences was established in 1941 together with the Academy of Sciences, in the building of the former State Wróblewski Library. In the inter-war period the Wróblewski Library was one of the largest Vilnius libraries (founded by lawyer Tadeusz Wróblewski): in 1941 the new Library inherited from it 163 thousand volumes, more than 35 thousand manuscripts, large collections of numismatics, cartography and artworks. Later it was supplemented by extensive collections from other libraries, public, religious and private – from The Synod of the Evangelical Reformers (founded in 1557), the Society of Lovers of Science, Roman Catholic and Russian Orthodox ecclesiastical seminaries and others. Presently its stocks count more than 3.5 mln items.

## Słuszki estate ㊼

At Kosciuškos St. 10, screened by newer houses, stands a large palace built in 1690–94 by Dominick Słuszko, voivode of Polock. It was noted for its stately late Baroque appearance. Noteworthy is an interesting Baroque pediment with a stucco bas-relief. Michelangelo Palloni and Pietro Perti are thought to be the authors of the decorations. In 1705 tsar Peter I stayed at the palace, and in 1794 the rebels' headquarters and canon foundry operated there. In 1833

Pediment of the main façade of the Słuszki estate

Słuszki estate. Ca.1869. Photo by Józef Czechowicz

Kosciuškos St. 36

the building was converted into a fortress, in the process it was radically altered, the spacious rooms were divided, the interior décor destroyed, and an additional floor built. In the 19th cent. it housed a prison.

Between the Słuszki estate and the Church of St. Peter and St. Paul suburban gardens stretched in earlier times, later built over with villas (today they are occupied mainly by embassies). The building of the present Embassy of Denmark (Kosciuškos St. 36) housed the headquarters of the Soviet general Ivan Cherniakhovsky in the summer of 1944. In this building the Soviet KGB, under a pretext of holding a council, arrested the leadership of the Polish underground army (Armia Krajowa) and the general "Wilk" (Aleksander Krzyżanowski).

Vileišis estate

Detail of the east façade of Vileišis' residential house

## Vileišis Estate ㊽

It is located at Antakalnio St. 4, close to the Church of St. Peter and St. Paul. The main house was built in 1904–06 by the Lithuanian businessman and public figure Petras Vileišis according to a design by engineer August Klein. It is one of the first buildings in Vilnius, for whose construction a rare material in Lithuania – concrete – was used. Beside the main house, closer to the street, stands a residential house, in which the first exhibition of Lithuanian art took place in 1907. In 1931 the buildings were donated to the Lithuanian Scolarly Society and the "Rytas" educational society. Later the Institutes of the Lithuanian Language and Lithuanian Literature and Folklore were established there.

Both buildings are neo-Baroque with some features of the Modernist (Jugend) style, particularly in the interior. Valuable collections related to Lithuanian studies, and artworks are held there.

Church of St. Peter
and St. Paul

## Church of St. Peter and St. Paul ㊾

It is the most exquisite Baroque monument in Vilnius (Antakalnio St. 1/1). Its interior décor – ca. 2,000 stucco statues – is unique in Europe.

According to tradition, a sanctuary of the pagan goddess of love Milda was located on this site. Since the times of Lithuania's Christianization a wooden church stood there, destroyed during the 1655–61 war with Moscow. The present Church of St. Peter and St. Paul was built by hetman Michael Casimir Pac to mark the liberation of Vilnius from Russians and his own escape from the hands of rebellious soldiers. Construction began in 1668 according to a project by architect Jan Zaor; until 1671 it was supervised by Zaor himself, and later by Gianbattista Frediani and others. The church acquired its present appearance in 1676; in 1671–1704 it was decorated with stucco moldings (sculptors Pietro Perti, Giovanni Maria Galli and others), and frescoes. Pac died in 1682 and did not see the church finished. In 1801–04 Giovanni Beretti and Nicolae Piano, from Milan, renovated the building and created a rococo pulpit. The altar holds an academicist painting "The Parting of St. Peter and St. Paul" by Franciszek Smuglewicz (1804). In 1953–89 this altar held the coffin of St. Casimir.

Detail of the interior –
a console

A square in front of the church is named after John Paul II in memory of the pope's visit to Lithuania and Vilnius.

From the outside the church looks austere and restrained. It is of a Latin cross design with a cupola and small twin towers. The church is three-nave: the side naves are transformed into chapels (two chapels under the towers have a circular plan). The façade is two-tiered, with columns and a balcony. Its Latin inscriptions correspond to the spirit of the Baroque era. Michael Casimir Pac had ordered to bury him under the threshold of the church and inscribe *Hic iacet peccator* (A sinner rests here) on the tombstone; his tombstone was split up by lightning in the late 17th cent., therefore a plaque with the inscription was transferred onto the wall, on the right side of the entry. Pac's humility is disproved by the fact that he found a way of perpetuating his name in another inscription above the balcony: *Regina Pacis funda nos in pace* (Queen of Peace,

Chandelier

Central nave

Detail of the interior

Altar of the Jesus
of Antakalnis

give us courage in peace). It is a Baroque conceit: the words "Queen of Peace" can be interpreted as "Queen of Pac". The coat-of-arms of the Pac family is set up above the entry.

The church is surrounded by a brick wall with arched niches (from the side of the courtyard) and four towers-chapels. On the north-east stands the Monastery of the Lateran Canons (1677–82), connected with the church by an arcade, above which a closed corridor is built on. On the left (northwest) façade is a peculiar primitivist painting representing the plague in Vilnius. Executed with oil on wood (1761), it was repainted many times.

The church interior is much more magnificent and diverse. Its sculptural groups are arranged in a complex way according to the principle of the "world theatre" (the spectator is God whose face is represented on the ridge of the cupola). Among them are biblical, historical, mythical and allegoric figures, representatives of various nations, social strata and professions, fantastic and demonic beings, plants, animals, heavenly bodies, military insignia, liturgical and daily objects. Walking clockwise from the church door, we find a baptistery, the Chapel of the Blessed Virgins, St. Augustine's Chapel, the west part of the transept with the altar of Mary the Compassionate, the east part of the transept with the altar of the Saviour's Five Wounds, St. Ursula's Chapel, Chapel of the Holy Warriors and a round chapel under the east tower. The narthex at the entry is decorated with an image of St. Christopher (coat-of-

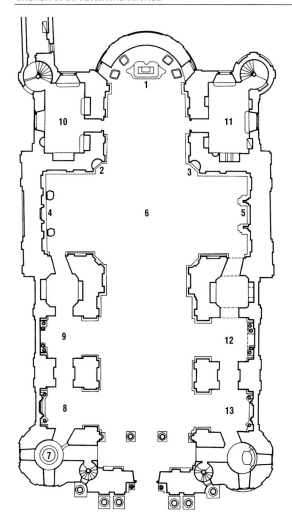

Plan of the Church

1. High altar
2. Altar of the Jesus of Antakalnis
3. Altar of St. Francis of Assisi
4. Altar of Mary the Compassionate
5. Altar of the Saviour's Five Wounds
6. Central section
7. Round chapel (former baptistery)
8. Chapel of the Blessed Virgins
9. St. Augustine's Chapel
10. West sacristy
11. East sacristy
12. St. Ursula's Chapel
13. Chapel of the Holy Warriors

Details of the interior

arms of Vilnius) and a skeleton with a scythe trampling down the symbols of earthly power. It is echoed by a dynamic sculpture of Christ Resurrected in the presbytery (the skeleton and Christ are separated by the entire space of the church). Another contrast to Christ is a serene sculpture of Mary on the other side of the presbytery. It is one of many examples of sculptures constituting an opposition in space. Another case is a relief work of St. Sebastian in the central nave: in front of it, on the other side of the nave, one sees an image of a centurion who had given an order to shoot arrows at the saint, and in the next relief work the same centurion is already converted, looking at the altar of Mary the Compassionate.

Noteworthy are many other Baroque sculptures and relief works. Sculptures of St. Peter and St. Paul are mainly arranged in groups – they constitute scenes bearing an allegoric meaning or telling a narrative. The baptistery and the Chapel of the Holy Warriors hold expressive figures of demons. In the Chapel of the Blessed Virgins evangelical virtues are represented: patience, humility, innocence and compassion (the latter figure is giving alms to a realistically modelled beggar). The arch consoles of St. Augustine's Chapel hold stylized elephant heads (the saint was born in Africa), and two girls' heads in front (traditionally regarded as a Lithuanian and a Pole). In the vault, the relief work of the apotheosis of St. Augustine is encircled by a sculptural crown from Lithuanian flowers. Beside is one of the most beautiful relief works in the church – Caritas, with two infants at her breast. A vertical relief work represents a tree of good and evil (with heads of a dragon among flowers and birds). In the west part of the transept one sees Christ stopping the arrows of plague threatening people; in the vault – episodes from the life of the Holy Virgin Mary and a crowd of angels playing the musical instruments. The famous painting of Mary also hangs there. In the east part angels are holding instruments of Christ's torture. St. Ursula's Chapel holds probably the

Sculpture of St. Mary Magdalen

Detail of the decoration of the entablature

Sculpture of Christ Resurrected

most remarkable statue in the church – St. Mary Magdalen (traditionally considered a portrait of Pietro Perti's wife); noteworthy is a panneau with a floral ornament of exquisite subtleness. The Chapel of the Holy Warriors contains valuable sculptures of St. Florian and St. Moor, a relief work on a battle theme with St. Casimir, and armed angels on cornices. The central nave above the arches holds allegories of evangelical blessings. Impressive is the composition of the cupola (angels among rays coming from the face of God). Four evangelists are represented on the wings of the cupola.

At the crossing of the transept and the presbytery, a 20th cent. altar is dominated by a wooden sculpture of the Jesus of Antakalnis with a wig of natural hair, considered miraculous (in 1700 it was brought from Rome in parts and finished in Vilnius). It was moved here from the Trinitarian Church in 1864. A marble chalice in the baptistery also dates from the 17th cent. A ship-shaped chandelier was manufactured by Liepaja artisans (1905).

The vault of the central nave is adorned by frescoes from the 2nd half of the 17th cent. representing episodes from the life of St. Peter.

Memorial to Lithuanian
independence fighters
killed in 1991

## Antakalnio Cemetery ㊿

It is situated in a hilly pine grove to the northeast of the Church of
St. Peter and St. Paul. Established in 1809, later it was greatly
expanded. Mostly soldiers (Russian, German and Polish) were
buried there. Today the cemetery has become a pantheon of the
Republic of Lithuania: there rest the independence fighters killed
on January 13th 1991 at the Television Tower, and border guards
killed in Medininkai on July 31st 1991. At their graves a monument
"Pieta" (sculptor Stanislovas Kuzma, 1995) has been erected.

Farther on stands a monument to Soviet soldiers killed in the
struggles against the Nazis (1951, reconstructed in 1976–84). On
the left communist leaders of Soviet Lithuania are buried (Justas
Paleckis, Antanas Sniečkus and others). Closer to the entry rest cul-
tural figures of the period of Soviet occupation – writers, artists,
musicians, theatre people and scientists: Janina Degutytė,
Augustinas Gricius, Adolfas Jucys, Kostas Korsakas, Stasys
Krasauskas, Eduardas Mieželaitis, Juozas Mikėnas, Antanas
Miškinis, Ieva Simonaitytė, Paulius Širvys, Jonas Švedas, Stasys
Vainiūnas, Antanas Venclova and others. Some literary and cultur-
al figures of a later period, including Lithuanian émigrés (Vytautas
Kavolis) are also buried there.

Monument "Pieta"

In the southwest part of the cemetery are the graves of Petras
Baublys, Teodor Bujnicki, Konstantinas Galkauskas, Kazys Inčiūra,
Romualdas Juknevičius, Stasys Matulaitis, Bronius Pundzius,
Merkelis Račkauskas, Vosylius Sezemanas and Justinas Vieno-
žinskis.

Gate of the Sapieha park

In another, so-called Saulės (St. Peter and St. Paul) Cemetery,
famous cultural figures Danielius Alseika, Jonas Kazlauskas,
Teodoras Valaitis, Józef Zawadski are buried.

## Sapieha estate and park ㉛

Between the Church of St. Peter and St. Paul and Antakalnio
Cemetery lies a large irregular plot with remnants of an ancient
estate (L. Sapiegos St. 3). The great hetman of the Grand Duchy
Casimir Sapieha built a palace on this site in 1691. It was magnificent, decorated with sculptures and frescoes created by masters

Sapieha estate. 1916.
Photo by Jan Bułhak

who had worked in the Church of St. Peter and St. Paul and St. Casimir's Chapel of the Cathedral. However, in the early 18th cent. the estate deteriorated and was further damaged during the 1794 uprising, until it was finally given over to a hospital in 1809 (in 1812 it housed a French hospital; at the present time it is also occupied by a hospital). In the 19th and 20th cent. the estate suffered various misfortunes. Among the surviving details are Baroque façades with stucco relief works by Pietro Perti, though transformed, and three Baroque gates. The park is the only one in Vilnius with features of a regular Baroque park.

## Church of Our Lord Jesus and the Trinitarian Monastery ㉒

Trinitarian Church

The Trinitarian Church of Our Lord Jesus (Antakalnio St. 27) is situated north of the Sapieha estate, on the former possessions of the Sapiehas. It was built by the efforts of Casimir Sapieha in 1694–1717; the interior sculptural décor was created by Pietro Perti in 1700–05. Twin towers, not quite harmonizing with the Baroque forms of the church, were built on in the 18th cent. and transformed later. In 1864 the church was converted into a Russian Orthodox church and severely damaged; in the 1920's it was partly renovated. On the façade frieze two Christian soldiers taken into captivity by the Muslims are represented (the main goal of the Trinitarian order was returning such captives to their homelands). The church has an impressive cupola, the interior is adorned with stucco relief works and sculptures – a large part of them has survived. Art historians consider the Church of Our Lord Jesus a "sister" to the Church of St. Peter and St. Paul, though the first one is more modest. Now it belongs to the ecclesiastical seminary.

Nearby stand buildings of the Trinitarian Monastery from the late 17th–18th cent. The Trinitarians were a missionary order. In the 18th cent. the order's collegium operated in the monastery, and a parish school was established there in 1726. In 1924 the buildings were converted into a university clinic. Since 1993 it houses the ecclesiastical seminary.

East of the church, Sapieha Park and Antakalnio Cemetery, stretch the Sapieginė Hills beloved by skiers. Antakalnio St. goes northwards to Valakampių grove and the Neris beach.

St. Faustine's House

## St. Faustine's House ⑤③

At Vinco Grybo St. 29a (close to the Trinitarian Church and Antakalnio Cemetery), the former house of the Congregation of the Holy Mother the Compassionate is situated. In 1924 and 1933–38, Sister Faustine (Maria Helena Kowalska, 1905–1938), a Catholic mystic, saint and the founder of the cult of God's Compassion, lived and wrote her diaries in this house.

## Užupis ⑤④ ⑤⑤

It is one of the oldest Vilnius suburbs on the right bank of the Vilnia, mentioned as early as the 15th cent. Užupis was inhabited mainly by craftsmen, particularly weavers, and since the 19th cent. – by minor officials. The north part of the suburb (present Filaretų and Krivių St.) belonged to the Russian Orthodox Fraternity of the Holy Spirit, thus priests and churchmen lived there. Since several overflow dams and dikes had been erected on the Vilnia, its banks were crowded with small enterprises, so-called water mills. For example, in 1524 Carol Weynart received a permit from Sigismund the Older to build a paper mill at the Vilnia in Užupis. The printer Mamonich also had a paper mill at the Vilnia.

Užupis can be reached by Bernardinų, Paplaujos or Užupio bridges over the Vilnia. In the Soviet period, many young artists took to this desolate old suburb and are now trying to turn in into the Monmartre of Vilnius. They hold yearly festivals of alternative art and fashion, celebrate calendar and other holidays, hold vari-

View of Užupis from Subačiaus St.

Paplaujos Bridge across the Vilnia

Detail of the façade
of the Honesti estate
(Užupio St. 7/1)

Banks of the Vilnia

ous actions and happenings, and have even proclaimed the
Republic of Užupis. From Užupis hillsides excellent view of the
Vilnius old town are exposed.

Malūnų St. is formed by a long building of the Užupis Bernardine
Convent (No. 3) – once its wall alongside the street was blind. The
convent was established in 1495 as the first women's convent in

Paplavų suburb.
1860's. Photo by
Józef Czechowicz

Lithuania. It did not have its own church, and the nuns would go
to mass to the Bernardine Church. In 1692 the convent was connected with the church with a gallery (in 1867 the gallery was
pulled down). During the 1794 uprising, wooden buildings of the
convent burned down, and the nuns began the construction of the
brick buildings that have survived into our times. In 1864 the convent was closed down. From 1876 to the First World War it
belonged to the Russian Orthodox Fraternity of the Holy Spirit;
later apartments were laid out.

At No. 2 lived (1934–36) Polish poet Konstanty Ildefons Gałczyński, who dedicated many lively, often humorous poems to
Lithuania's capital and the Vilnia.

At Užupio St. 7/1 stands the Honesti family estate designed in the
late Classical style (apparently built in 1828–41).

Bernardine Cemetery

Behind the gate, in a courtyard (Užupio St. 17a), stands the Church of St. Bartholomew, probably the smallest in Vilnius. In 1788 a Classical brick church replaced the earlier wooden one. During the 1794 uprising it was damaged and rebuilt as late as 1824 according to a project by architect Karol Podczaszyński in the eclectic style. A belfry was erected in 1881. The church presently serves for the Vilnius Belorussian community.

By Polocko St. (along which Russian merchants used to come to Vilnius) one can reach Bernardinų Cemetery established in 1810 (a chapel was built in 1828). In this cemetery rest university professors, scientists, artists, among others – culture historian Michał Brensztejn, natural scientists Józef and Stanisław Bonifacy Jundziłł, mathematician Zachary Niemczewski, artists Vytautas Kairiūkštis (and his sister, art critic Halina Kairiūkštytė-Jacinienė), Bolesław and Kanuty Rusiecki, Wincenty Śłędziński, photographers Stanisław Fleury and Józef Czechowicz.

Gate on Užupio St.
and the Church
of St. Bartholomew

By Batoro St. through the Belmonto Grove frequented by the Philomats and Philarets, one can reach an impressive monument of nature – Pūčkorių precipice at the Vilnia. The street leads to the Naujoji Vilnia suburb.

On the opposite bank of Vilnia river, at the Subačius St. end, lays the Markučiai suburb. Surrounded by old oaks, lindens and pin-trees, on a high hill stands here the former homestead of the poet's Alexander Pushkin son Grigory (1835–1905). Alexander Pushkin literary museum operates in this Russian landlords house.

Markučiai estate
and park

Bust of
Alexander Pushkin
near the estate building

Gedimino Avenue

Sculpture
"The Feast of Muses"

## Gedimino Avenue and its surroundings ⑤⑥

Construction of the present main street of Vilnius began in 1836. It
begins at the Castle Hill and follows a northwest direction connecting the Cathedral, Municipality, Lukiškių and Independence
Squares. The straight, not very wide avenue is almost 2 km long
and ends in a bridge to the Žvėrynas suburb. It was initially called
St. George Avenue, and later – Mickiewicz, Gedimino, Stalin and
Lenin Avenue, depending on Lithuania's political situation. In
1989 it was once more named after the founder of the city,
Gediminas (that name had been first assigned to it by the Lithu-

Gedimino Ave. 1

Opposite p.:

View of Tilto Street,
farther – the Church of
St. George the Martyr

Building of the
Lithuanian Writers'
Union (Sirvydo St. 6)

Interior of the building

anian administration in 1939). 20th cent. buildings serving the administrative, cultural and commercial purpose, dominate the avenue: it is a representational part of the Lithuanian capital.

A building (Gedimino Ave. 1), which housed the "Sajūdis" headquarters in the period of independence struggles, faces the Cathedral Square. Its ground floor is occupied by "Literatų" café (replacing Rudnicki's café "Liter A" frequented by intellectuals, which operated before the Second World War). To the northwest of Gedimino Ave. an old picturesque Tilto St. branches off.

No. 3 – the Palace of the Academy of Sciences (earlier – the Bank Palace), an early 20th cent. Historicist building.

No. 4 – National Drama Theatre. Built in 1981 on the site of an older early 20th cent. theatre building (architects Algimantas and Vytautas Nasvytis). The sculpture above the entry is called "The Feast of Muses" and shows figures of Drama, Tragedy and Comedy (sculptor Stanislovas Kuzma, 1981).

No. 7 – Central Post Office, a late 19th cent. Historicist building. In 1969 architects Algimantas and Vytautas Nasvytis reconstructed the building in a more modern style, retaining its old façade.

Behind the Post Office (Sirvydo St. 6) stands a stylish neo-Baroque palace (1839–68) that once belonged to Hipolit Korwin-Milewski, and later – to Count Anthony Tyszkiewicz and Countess Ogińska. In 1944 it was given over to the Lithuanian Writers' Union. The interior boasts a richly decorated staircase, tile stoves, elaborate pieces of furniture, chandeliers and wood carvings. The building still houses the Lithuanian Writers' Union.

186  SAVIVALDYBĖS SQUARE SURROUNDINGS

## Savivaldybės (Municipality) Square surroundings ⑤⑦

At the Municipality (formerly Ožeškienės, Černiachovskio) Square
stands the Church of St. George the Martyr (Sirvydo St. 4), whose
east end faces the Post Office and the Writers' Union. It was built
in 1506 for the Carmelite monks who had settled in the territory of
the Radziwiłł Estate and for whose maintenance Vilnius Voivode
Michael Radziwiłł allotted land and funding. Formerly Gothic, in
1750–55 the church was restored according to a project by Franz
Ignatius Hoffer and acquired some features of late Baroque and
rococo. The façade is decorated by pilasters, volutes and relief-
work décor; the eastern pediments are also elegant and picturesque. The vaults and the presbytery are abundantly covered in
mural paintings (1775; restored in 1908). Nearby stand the
17th–18th buildings of the Carmelite Monastery. The monastery
had a rich archive and library, a study centre operated there, and
the monks were distinguished by their pastoral activity. In
1797–1944 it housed the Vilnius Ecclesiastical Seminary. After the
closing of the monastery, its ancillary buildings were converted
into residential houses. Presently part of the monastery is occupied
by the Book Chamber, and the church – by a book depository.

Further to the north towards Žaliasis Bridge, at Vienuolio St. 1,
rises the large building of the Opera and Ballet Theatre (architect
Nijolė Bučiūtė, 1974). It has 1149 seats. The walls of the building are
made of glass and decorated with brass plates. In 1974 a monument to one of the founding fathers of Lithuanian opera, the celebrated tenor Kipras Petrauskas, was erected in front of the theatre
(sculptor Gediminas Jokūbonis, 1974). Closer to the Neris, on Goš-
tauto St. 1, a neo-Classical building (1907) that once housed the
Vilnius Society of Lovers of Science, is located.

In front of the Municipality Square, on the other side of Gedimino
Ave., stands a group of buildings in the style of Functionalism and
Constructivism dating from the inter-war period: a former Palace
of the Post Savings Bank (No. 12), a former bank (No. 14), and a former House of Commerce of the Jabłkowski brothers (No. 18/13).

Having turned southwards along Vilniaus St., we come across several places related with the memory of famous people and historic
events. At Vilniaus St. No. 12 Mikalojus Konstantinas Čiurlionis
was a frequent guest. Janka Kupala had an apartment at No. 14.

Church of St. George
the Martyr

Detail of the fresco
in the church

Monument to
Kipras Petrauskas

Building of the Opera
and Ballet Theatre

Former St. George
Hotel
(Gedimino Ave. 20/1)

No. 21 housed an editorial office of the Belorussian newspaper *Naša Dolia* (1906), where Anton and Jan Luckievich wrote the first documents of the Belorussian national revival. In No. 25 Jonas Basanavičius died in 1927 (February 16th, the day of his death, coincided with the anniversary of the Independence Act). This

building also housed a musical school, where the famous violinist Jasha Heifetz studied in 1905–09.

South of Gedimino Ave., in front of the former House of Commerce of the Jabłkowski brothers, a short Jogailos St. branches off. On its corner stands the former St. George Hotel (No. 20/1) built in the late 19th cent. according to a design by Tadeusz Rostworowski,

Gedimino Ave. 14

Vilniaus St. 21

Pylimo St. 4

Monument to Sugihara,
a consul of Japan
in Lithuania

Façade of the hotel and café "Neringa" ("Scandic Hotel Neringa")

Monument to Žemaitė

Church of St. Jacob and St. Philip

and considered the best in Vilnius for a long time. Jogailos St. leads to Pylimo St. that bounds the old town from the west and leads toward the railway and bus terminals. At the crossing of Pylimo and Pamėnkalnio streets stands a monument to writer Petras Cvirka (sculptor Juozas Mikėnas, 1959). Farther apart, at the crossing of Pylimo and Kalinausko streets (in a little square), the first monument to Frank Zappa in the world was erected by his fans (sculptor Konstantinas Bogdanas, 1995). At Pylimo St. 4 is a house of the small Vilnius Jewish community, at Pamėnkalnio St. 12 is the Jewish Museum, in front of which stands a monument to Sugihara, a consul of Japan in Lithuania, who saved about 2,000 Jews from the Nazis.

Gedimino Ave. 23 houses the hotel and café "Neringa". The café was appointed in 1959 (architects Algimantas and Vytautas Nasvytis), in the times of Soviet occupation it was frequented by Vilnius intellectuals; its décor has retained the typical style of the "thaw" period. On the same side of the avenue Žemaitės Square with a monument to the writer erected in 1970 (sculptor Petras Aleksandravičius) is located. In front of it, on a by-street farther apart from the avenue, stands a house (No. 34), in the garret of which poet Joseph Brodsky once stayed in 1970; the garret is described in his poem "The Lithuanian Nocturne".

## Lukiškių Square and its surroundings ⑤⑧ ⑤⑨ ⑥⓪ ⑥①

It is one of the largest Vilnius squares (4 ha). On its north side stands a twin-tower Baroque Church of St. Jacob and Philip and the Dominican Monastery (Lukiškių Sq. 10). The church was built on this site in 1624, and the present building dates from the late 17th–18th cent. It is a single-nave church with cylindrical vaults; an image of the miraculous painting of the high altar (18th cent.) occupies the niche above the portico. The niches hold wooden 18th cent. statues of St. Hyacinth and St. Dominic. During Soviet times plans were advanced to demolish the church; later it was abandoned, and in 1992 it was returned to its parishioners. A painting of the Holy Mother the Compassionate (Lukiškių Mother of God), famous for its miracles since the 17th cent., was also returned to the church.

The monastery was established in the 18th cent. In 1723 an almshouse was built with funding by Steponas Sliznia, a scribe of the Ašmena land, who assigned 4,000 Lithuanian gold coins for the maintenance of 12 poor people; this marks the beginning of the monastery hospital, which is the oldest hospital in Lithuania. The Dominican monks ran the hospital, until it became the first secular city hospital in 1808 (established in the monastery building). One of the leaders of the 1863 uprising, Zygmunt Sierakowski, spent his last days at St. Jacob's Hospital. The monastery was reopened in 1993.

In the middle of the 19th cent. a suburban waste ground stretched out on the site of the present square; in 1863 executions of the rebels took place there. In memory of the rebels, a plaque with an inscription "1863" was set up in 1929, and moved closer to the church from the centre of the square in 1936. Since 1904 the square was famous for St. Casimir's fairs. In 1952 a monument to Lenin was erected there (dismantled in 1991). A photo of dismantling the monument figured prominently in the world press and became perhaps the most eloquent symbol of the fall of Communism.

To the west of the square stands an old (still operating) Lukiškių prison, where in the times of the tsars, in the inter-war period, as well as during the Nazi and Soviet occupations, fighters against the regime were imprisoned; many people who did not take part in any political activity but had fallen in disgrace with the occupational regimes, also suffered there. On the south side of the square (Gedimino Ave. 40), a former District Court Palace is located (1890). During Nazi times it housed the Gestapo, and during the time of Soviet occupation – the KGB. Presently in this building (Aukų St. 2a) a unique museum of Genocide Victims has been established. On its façade names of the resistance fighters killed in the building are carved, and nearby a small monument – a pyramid of fieldstones collected in various places of Lithuania, is erected.

"Montwiłł colony" from Tumo-Vaižganto St.

District Court Palace

Detail of the façade of the House of Scientists

Muslim cemetery in
Lukiškės suburb.
Photo by Jan Bułhak

Between Lukiškių Square and the Neris stands a building of extraordinary size in the style of Socialist Realism – the House of Scientists (Tumo-Vaižganto St. 9/1). Its tower with a belvedere and a spire imitates the Admiralty building in St. Petersburg. The house was built in 1950; it was home to Juozas Balčikonis, Juozas Mikėnas and other Lithuanian cultural figures. Closer to the square, J. Tumo-Vaižganto St., J. Savickio St. and Kražių St. form a triangular block, the so-called Montwiłł colony. It is a complex of 22 residential buildings (1911–13), one of the first residential districts in Vilnius. Some of the houses have features of the Modernist style, some are neo-Gothic; their bizarre, asymmetrical, strictly individual façades and volumes create an architectural landmark quite unusual in Vilnius. The block was named after the financier and public figure Józef Montwiłł, the founder of urban development in Vilnius. In the vicinity (closer to Žvėryno Bridge, on Mečetės St.) once stood a wooden mosque and Muslim graves destroyed during Soviet times.

Along the eastern edge of Lukiškių Square runs Vasario 16-osios St. On the western side of its continuation – Tauro St. – looms the Tauras Hill, erroneously related with the legend about Gediminas' hunt. Its takes its name from the French cartographer Bouffal; Bouffal's name was interpreted as "buffalo", i.e. "tauras" in Lithuanian. The real name of the hill is Pamėnkalnis. A broad panorama of the city is exposed from the hill. At its edge, on the Tauro St. 5, stands a Constructivist students' hostel built in the inter-war period. Czesław Miłosz, a Nobel Prize winner in 1980, lived there while studying in Vilnius (1929–34).

On this street (No. 10) stands a house from the 1930's with memorial plaques to writers Vincas Krėvė, Vincas Mykolaitis-Putinas and Balys Sruoga. In the same house (on the ground floor from the courtyard) Nadezhda Mandelshtam, a Russian dissident writer, the widow of poet Osip Mandelshtam, stayed in 1974, and in 1975 – the famous fighter for human rights Andrei Sakharov who had come to Vilnius to defend his friend Sergei Kovaliov, taken to court for his support to Lithuanian resistance fighters. At that time Sakharov was supposed to receive the Nobel peace prize in Oslo, therefore his visit was widely publicized in the world and contributed to the collapse of the Soviet empire.

V. Mykolaitis-Putinas'
memorial museum
(Tauro St. 10–3)

Students' hostel
(Tauro St. 5)

Seimas
(Parliament) Palace

## Nepriklausomybės (Independence) Square ⑥②

In this square, at Gedimino Ave. 53, stands the Seimas Palace
(architects Algimantas and Vytautas Nasvytis and Robertas
Stasėnas, 1982). The Palace entered Lithuania's and world history
in 1990–91. On March 11th, the Act "For the Restoration of an
Independent State of Lithuania" marking the beginning of the collapse of the Soviet Union, was proclaimed there. On January 13th
1991, the Soviet Army was planning to attack the Lithuanian
Parliament, but was discouraged by the adamant resistance of the
people and members of parliament who defended the Palace. It is
commemorated by fragments of the barricades and memorial
signs at the Palace.

National Martynas
Mažvydas Library

The National Martynas Mažvydas Library (1963) is located next to
the Seimas Palace (Gedimino Ave. 51).

Žvėryno Bridge across the
Neris, farther – the
Russian Orthodox Church
of the Apparition of the
Holy Mother of God

## Žvėrynas ⑥③ ⑥④

A suburb on the right bank of the Neris, presently in the process of
merging with the city centre. Its main street (Mickevičiaus) is a
continuation of Gedimino Ave.

Since the 16th cent. Žvėrynas belonged to the Radziwiłłs, who maintained a hunting preserve there. Aurochses, elks and other kinds of
game lived in the forest; hence the name of the suburb ("Žvėrynas"
means "menagerie"). In the 19th cent. a forest grew in this area. In
1893 its proprietor, merchant Martinson, parcelled out the whole

Kenessa

area and began to sell the plots to citizens. Since that time wooden and brick villas and summerhouses went up in the district. Today Žvėrynas is becoming a prestigious residential part of the capital.

The first wooden bridge connecting Žvėrynas with the present Gedimino Ave. was built in 1892. The present metal bridge (91 m) with stone piers dates from 1906. It is used only for pedestrians and light traffic; another bridge further down has been built for heavy traffic. At the bridge (Mickevičiaus St. 1) stands the Russian Orthodox Znamenskaya Church, or Church of the Apparition of the Holy Mother of God (1903). Its Byzantine cupolas completing the panorama of Gedimino Ave. form a kind of opposition to the Cathedral at the other end of the avenue (paradoxically, the Eastern church is on its west side, and the Cathedral on the east side). Ca. 400 m away from the bridge, at the south end of Vytauto St., lies a round stone with a symbol of the Gediminas Columns, apparently a landmark of the lands of the Grand Duke in the 15th cent.

South of Mickevičiaus St., at Liubarto St. 6, stands a Kenessa (Karaite sanctuary) built in the Moorish style in 1922. The Karaites are a small religious and national community brought from the Crimea by Vytautas. Their language is Turkic, and their religion – a branch of Judaism (they adhere to the Old Testament, but do not accept the Talmud). The community has survived until our days.

## Vingio park ⑥⑤ ⑥⑥

On the other side of Žvėrynas, in the Neris loop, stretches a large Vingio pine forest (160 ha) surrounded by the river from three sides. In the 15th–16th cent. it belonged to the Radziwiłłs, later to Bishop Ignacy Massalski, and afterwards to Governor General of Vilnius Leontii Bennigsen who built a sumptuous summer residence here. In *War and Peace* Leo Tolstoy mentions that on June 13th 1812, on the occasion of maneuvres of the Russian army, Bennigsen was planning to throw a feast at his residence, with the participation of Alexander I. For that occasion a special pavilion had been built; unfortunately, it collapsed a day before the feast. Architect Michael Schulz who had designed it could not bear the shame and drowned himself in the Neris. Anyway, the pavilion was appointed and a feast thrown. When it was in full swing, an envoy brought a message to the tsar that Napoleon had crossed the Nemunas. Before long French soldiers arrived in Vilnius. Incidentally, they converted the palace into a war hospital which later burned down together with all its patients.

At the edge of the park, at Čiurlionio St. 91, stands a Classical chapel built by Governor General Nikolai Repnin for his wife in 1799–1800. Next to the chapel, German soldiers cemetery (soldiers of other nationalities were buried there too) is under reconstruction now. Nearby, at Čiurlionio St. 29, the new buildings of the Astronomical Observatory of Vilnius University are located (1930's).

Vingio Park is a beloved rest place of Vilniusites. In 1960 a roofed grandstand with a platform for song festivals was erected there; it became a site of concerts and festivals. Mass meetings that marked the beginning of the struggle for the restoration of independence took place on the site in 1988.

## Jono Basanavičiaus Street and its surroundings ⑥⑦ ⑥⑧

A street mostly lined with representational buildings, which marks the beginning of the way leading from Vilnius to the west, towards Trakai, Kaunas and the Baltic Sea. It rises from the crossing of Pylimo and Trakų streets uphill. On its highest point stands the Russian Orthodox Church of St. Michael and St. Constantine (Basanavičius St. 27) built on the occasion of the 300th anniversary of the Romanov dynasty (1913).

No. 13 – Theatre Palace, one of the most significant early 20th cent. buildings of cultural function in Vilnius (1912–13, architects Wacław Michniewicz and Aleksander Parczewski). Its style refers to Baroque and even Romanesque architecture. In 1925–29 it housed the Polish theatre "Reduta" led by Juliusz Osterwa. In 1948–74, an opera and ballet theatre operated in the building; presently it houses the Russian Drama Theatre.

No. 16 – a neo-Gothic house (1897–1900). At the beginning of the First World War a Lithuanian high school was established here.

No. 18. In 1917–23 the famous French writer Romain Gary (Roman Kacew, 1914–80) lived in this house; a memorial plaque is set up on it.

No. 19 – Bulota house. It belonged to the Lithuanian public figure, lawyer Andrius Bulota, killed by the Nazis in 1941. In 1914–15 writer Žemaitė lived there.

Close to the Romanov Church, a cemetery of Evangelical Reformers was established in 1800. In the 1950's it was turned into a park; only a Classical mausoleum of the eminent surgeon Jan Fryderyk Niszkowski remained (1816 or 1819). It is thought that in this cemetery the fighter against the tsar's regime Szymon Konarski, executed in 1839, was buried; on the site where he had been shot down, a memorial stone was erected in 1924 (to the southwest of the cemetery, close to Vivulskio St.)

Theatre Palace

Detail of
Basanavičiaus St. 18

No. 44/43 – the city's guards house. A building of the late Classical (Empire) style (1819), built according to a typical project of the tsarist times (another guards house built according to the same design stands on Liepkalnio St.); towers marking the limit of the city used to stand nearby. There is a platform on which soldiers used to line up on the street side, and two rooms for officers and soldiers inside.

On the corner of S. Konarskio and Jovaro streets stands a slender Baroque Chapel of St. Hyacinth. It was built by the Dominican monks in 1762 (St. Hyacinth was a 13th cent. Dominican missionary). The dilapidated chapel was renovated in 1843, 1901 and 1998; during the renovation in 1901, a new brass statue of the saint was erected (sculptor Boleslaw Balzukiewicz).

At Vivulskio St. 18 the office of the Jewish Scholarly Institute YIVO (1933) used to stand. Its building did not survive. After the Second World War YIVO was moved to New York; part of the institute's collections has remained in Vilnius.

Chapel of St. Hyacinth

Žaliasis (Green) Bridge

## Žaliasis (Green) Bridge ⑥⑨

The oldest Vilnius bridge across the Neris, connecting Vilniaus and Kalvarijų streets. It was built by the Vilnius castle keeper Ulrich Hozius (1536). This wooden bridge was roofed, with shops. It was destroyed and rebuilt several times; in 1739 it was painted green (hence its name). A metal bridge built in 1894 was blown up in 1944 and restored in 1952. It is one of the few Lithuanian bridges adorned with sculptures – on its ends stand sculpture groups in the style of Socialist Realism symbolizing agriculture, industry, education and army (sculptors Juozas Mikėnas, Bronius Pundzius and others, 1952).

## Church of St. Archangel Raphael and its surroundings ⑦⓪ ⑦①

The Church of St. Archangel Raphael and the Jesuit Monastery (Šnipiškių St. 1) stands at the Neris riverside, at Žaliasis Bridge, in the Šnipiškių suburb. Once a road to Courland and Pskov started at this place. It is an elegant late Baroque monument (1702–30), made even more attractive by an asymmetrical monastery ensemble (1713–30). The towers date from the middle of the 18th cent., they end in rococo domes with lanterns. The church and the monastery belonged to the Jesuits. The monastery was intended

Church of St. Archangel Raphael

Raduszkiewicz estate

for monks with 10 years of service experience seeking to become professed Jesuits, i.e. to make the last ceremonial vows. Monks wishing to attain the highest stage of professed Jesuits had to spend 7 years in this home of the 3rd probation. After the abolishment of the Jesuit order, in 1773 it was given over to the Piusite monks, and later housed soldiers' barracks and an ammunition warehouse. In 1860 the church was returned to the Catholics. The

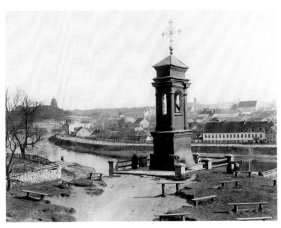

Chapel in Šnipiškės. 1860's. Photo by Józef Czechowicz

high altar holds a painting "St. Archangel Raphael" by Szymon Czechowicz (18th cent.). There are more valuable paintings; noteworthy are the pews from the 1st half of the 18th cent. moved here from the Bernardine Church.

On a small hill by the church once stood a chapel with a statue "Jesus Carrying a Cross" (Jesus of Šnipiškės), which attracted huge crowds of pilgrims (it was pulled down in the Soviet period).

In front of the church (on the other side of the street, Kalvarijų 1/2) stands an intricate Historicist Raduszkiewicz estate. It was built by medical doctor Hilary Raduszkiewicz in 1894–1900. Presumably, his taste was responsible for the bizarre appearance of the building (predominantly neo-Gothic). In 1962–63 part of the palace was pulled down, and in 1984–85 it was reconstructed.

Gate of the Calvary
road and one of the
chapels

## Vilnius Calvary ⑦⓶

The long Kalvarijų Street leads to the Jeruzalė suburb situated on a
hilly terrain, named thus because of the Stations of the Cross located there that used to attract many pilgrims. The creator of the
Calvary road was Bishop Jerzy Białłozor. Construction began in
1662, and in 7 years the Calvary Church of the Discovery of the
Holy Cross (Kalvarijų St. 225) and 35 wooden Stations of the Cross,
imitating the Road of Christ's Passions in Jerusalem, were built. It
was an expression of gratitude to God for the liberation of the
country from the Muscovites. It is the second oldest and once the
most famous Calvary in Lithuania, revered by pilgrims and processions of believers. After the wooden chapels burned down, 19
brick Baroque chapels, 7 wooden and one brick gates and a bridge
across the Baltupis rivulet renamed by the biblical name of Cedron
were constructed in the 18th cent. In 1963, most of the chapels were
blown up by the order of the Soviet authorities (only 4 have
remained). However, people continued marking off and tending to
the sites where the chapels stood, and the tradition of visiting them
has never been broken. At the present time the Vilnius Calvary is
under reconstruction; seven chapels were consecrated in 2000.

Calvary Church

The late Baroque church was rebuilt in the 18th cent. The central
nave is decorated with 18th cent. mural paintings, the sacristy –
with 18th cent. stucco relief works. A rococo pulpit and baptistery
deserve to be mentioned separately. At the church stands an 18th
cent. building of the monastery of Dominican observants.

## Trinapolis ⑦⓷

Walking along the road of the Stations of the Cross and looking in
the direction of the Neris from the hills, a view of the Church of the
Holy Trinity and the Trinitarian Monastery (Verkių St. 70) in a valley is exposed. Bishop Constantine Brzostowski settled Trinitarian
monks on this site in 1700; hence the name of the settlement:
Trinapolis is a city of Trinitarians.

Construction is thought to have taken place in 1695–1722 (apparently under architect Pietro Putini). In 1750–60 Trinapolis was
reconstructed in the late Baroque style. Though the interior décor
was destroyed, valuable architectural forms survived. The single-
nave church is built along an original plan (a cross in a rectangle).
It was a summer residence of Vilnius bishops.

In 1948 the church was closed, the monastery buildings housed a hospital, and later a tourist centre. In 1992 the buildings were returned to parishioners. A novitiate has been established in the renovated rooms, a house for prayer retreats is operating.

Verkiai tavern

## Ensemble of the Verkiai estate ⑭

The town of Verkiai is known since 1387. At that time it was the property of the Grand Duke (according to tradition, a child was found in an eagle's nest, who later became a pagan priest Lizdeika, the forefather of the Radziwiłł family). After Lithuania's Christianization, Jogaila donated Verkiai to the bishops of Vilnius who ruled it until 1794. The Verkiai estate forms a triaxial ensemble with Trinapolis and the Calvary.

In 1780, Bishop Ignacy Massalski settled in Verkiai; he commissioned Laurynas Stuoka-Gucevičius to reconstruct an earlier palace (the general plan and maintenance buildings were designed by Martin Knackfuss). The palace became one of the most valuable Classical buildings in Lithuania and was called "the Versailles of Vilnius". Duke Ludwig Wittgenstein, who bought Verkiai in 1839, ordered that the central building of the palace be pulled down. The maintenance buildings, many smaller buildings and a picturesque 36 ha park have remained. Since 1960 the ensemble belongs to the Lithuanian Academy of Sciences and is gradually renovated.

Detail of the eastern maintenance building of the Verkiai Palace

The most magnificent building is the eastern maintenance building (Žaliųjų Ežerų St. 49), in which the interiors of the Wittgenstein times (2nd half of the 19th cent.) have been restored. Noteworthy

Eastern maintenance building of the Verkiai Palace

Detail of the ceiling
of the former
billiard room

Interior of the eastern
maintenance building

is the western maintenance building of a moderate Classical style, an inn and pavilion designed by Stuoka-Gucevičius, as well as a villa, a water mill, an ice-cellar, greenhouses etc. An elegant administrative building of the estate (probably a tavern designed by Stuoka-Gucevičius) is located on Kalvarijų St. Situated on two terraces, the park consisted of two parts – the upper and the great park. Trees of ca. 30 varieties grow there, there are several ponds. A view of Vilnius is exposed from a steep slope.

6 km northeast of Verkiai (ca. 16 km from the city centre) lies a beautiful reservation of Žalieji ežerai (Green Lakes). It consists of Lake Kryžiuočių (56 ha), in which, according to tradition, a platoon of Teutonic knights drowned, Lake Gulbinas (35 ha) and Lake Mažasis Gulbinas (10 ha). The green colour of the lakes was attributed to the layers of chalk on their bottom, but it mostly comes from the reflection of steep woody slopes.

## Jewish cemetery ⑦⑤

The first Jewish cemetery in Vilnius was established in the 15th cent. in the Šnipiškės suburb (in front of the Gediminas Castle, on the other side of the Neris), where the Palace of Concerts and Sport now stands. It was destroyed by Soviet authorities in 1949–50. The second cemetery was situated in Užupis in 1828–1943; it was destroyed in the 1960's. The present cemetery is located in the Šeškinė suburb. The grave of the Gaon of Vilnius, at which believers leave votive messages, was moved there from Šnipiškės. The mausoleum of the Gaon family holds the ashes of Ger Tsedek (the legendary Count Valentin Potocki who converted to Judaism in 1749 and was burned at a stake). Nearby rest outstanding rabbis, public figures, literary people (Shmuel Fünn and others), medical doctor Tsemach Shabad, some martyrs of the ghetto. There is a memorial stone for children killed in the ghetto.

Grave of the Gaon
of Vilnius

## Paneriai Memorial ⑦⑥

In 1940 the Russian army began setting up a fuel repository in the Paneriai forest. At the outbreak of the Second World War, in July 1941, this forest turned into a mass killing site. Ten stone-lined pits and two trenches became the place where the majority of Vilnius Jews, Russian prisoners of war, several thousand Polish intellectu-

als, priests, underground fighters, as well as many Lithuanians, found a place of eternal rest. In 1943–44 Germans shot people in Higher Paneriai, among them Belorussian Jews, prisoners of the Vilnius ghetto and others.

Jewish cemetery in the Šnipiškės suburb. 1937. Photo by Jan Bułhak

Monument of the Paneriai Memorial

The first monument on this site (Agrastų St. 15) was erected in 1948, but dismantled in 1952 (probably because of a Yiddish inscription), to be replaced by a new one. Since 1960 a museum is operating in Paneriai. In 1985 a memorial was set up. In 1989–93 several more monuments commemorating the tragedy of Paneriai were erected.

## Television Tower ⑦

Built in 1980, it has a height of 326 m (higher than the Eiffel Tower). A sky-high "Paukščių takas" café is open in the tower.

The tower entered Lithuania's history on January 13th 1991, when fighters for independence were killed while defending it. A small museum is dedicated to their memory.

Television Tower

## Naujoji Vilnia ⑧

An industrial suburb to the south of the city centre, at a railway to Moscow and St. Petersburg. A neo-Gothic Church of St. Casimir in Naujoji Vilnia was built in 1911.

In the Stalinist era (1940–41 and 1944–53) Lithuanian citizens were deported to the Siberia by this railway. In June 1941 alone, ca. 30,000 deportees passed the Naujoji Vilnia station; the majority of them perished far from their homeland. A cross was erected in their memory at the railway in the central square (sculptor Vidmantas Gylikis, 1991).

1.5 km west of Naujoji Vilnia lies Rokantiškių cemetery, where several Lithuanian cultural figures, such as Petras Juodelis, Juozas Keliuotis, Bronius Untulis and Vincas Žilėnas, are buried.

There is a hill with remains of a castle in Rokantiškės. It is thought that one of the oldest castles in Lithuania dating from the 12th–13th cent. once stood there. It belonged to the Gasztold family, king Sigismund August and the Pac family; it was burned down in 1655 and not rebuilt afterwards.

## Major museums in Vilnius

### Vilnius Picture Gallery (Chodkiewicz Palace), Didžioji St. 4

Exhibits early Lithuanian art (16th–19th cent.) – painting, graphic art, sculpture. Concerts are held in the palace (in summer in the courtyard).

### Museum of Applied Art (The Old Arsenal), Arsenalo St. 3

Collections of 14th–20th Lithuanian and foreign applied art and Lithuanian applied art created after the Second World War are collected in the museum. Until 2003 the museum presents an exhibition "Christianity in Lithuanian Art", whose important part is the treasury of the Vilnius Cathedral. Temporary exhibitions and concerts are also held there.

### Gallery of Foreign Art (Radziwiłł Palace), Vilniaus St. 22

It collects and exhibits 16th–19th cent. West European (Italian, Flemish, Spanish etc.) painting and graphic art. 18th cent. brass engravings – 165 portraits of the Radziwiłł family – are on display in one of its halls. A permanent exhibition of indigenous Australian and Oceanian art (a collection of Genovaitė Kazokienė) is also open.

### National Museum (the New Arsenal), Arsenalo St. 1

Exhibits of Lithuanian history and ethnography. The past of the Grand Duchy of Lithuania is widely represented – iconography, numismatics, sphragistics, crafts, trades, various historical objects. There are departments of the tsarist occupation and the independent Lithuanian state in 1918–40. A unique collection of the history of the Freemasonry. Ethnographic exhibits represent daily life and folk art from all regions of Lithuania. Temporary exhibitions are held.

### Archaeology exhibition of the National Museum (the north building of the Old Arsenal), Arsenalo St. 3a

The first hall exhibits archaeological finds covering the period in which the territory of Lithuania was initially settled – the 11th mill. BC – to AD. The second hall holds exhibits from the 1st millennium to the formation of the Lithuanian state in the 13th cent. The exponents are supplemented by reconstructed jewelry and costumes.

### Gediminas Castle (Tower of the Higher Castle), Arsenalo St. 5

The exhibition narrates the history of the Vilnius castles. There is a survey site atop the tower.

### Bastion of the defensive wall, Bokšto St. 20/18

Exhibition of defensive fortifications and weaponry.

### Museum of Theatre, Music and Cinema, Vilniaus St. 41

Exhibition dedicated to the history of Lithuanian theatre, music and cinema.

### The House of Signatories, Pilies St. 26

In this house the Act of February 16th was signed in 1918; material related with the memory of the signatories of this act is on display.

### The Museum of Genocide Victims, Aukų St. 2a

This museum, rare in Europe, is established in a KGB prison. Prison cells, torture rooms, interrogation rooms, a prison library, a library of confiscated literature, as well as exhibits from the former museum of "the Tchekists' glory".

### The Jewish Museum, Pamėnkalnio St. 12, Naugarduko St. 10

Objects of the Jewish written history, religious rituals and daily life, as well as objects testifying to the Holocaust, and iconographic material.

### Alexander Pushkin Memorial Museum, Subačiaus St. 124

The museum is located in the estate of the poet's son Grigory (1835–1905) in Markučiai. A wooden estate house with an authentic interior and surroundings reflects the life of Russian landowners of the late 19th cent. The museum has some objects that belonged to Alexander Pushkin, as well as the material related with poets Taras Shevchenko, Janka Kupala, Jakub Kolas, Pavel Antokolski.

Adam Mickiewicz Memorial Apartment, Bernardinų St. 11
Located in the apartment where the poet lived in 1822.

## Galleries

"Akademija" Gallery, Pilies St. 44/2
Amber gallery, Šv. Mykolo St. 8
"Arka" Gallery, Aušros Vartų St. 7
Contemporary Art Centre, Vokiečių St. 2
Gallery "Kairė-dešinė", Latako St. 3
Gallery of medals, Šv. Jono St. 11
Gallery of Russian Art, Bokšto St. 4/2
"Lietuvos aidas" Gallery, Šv. Ignoto St. 6
Prospekto Gallery, Gedimino Ave. 43
"Vartai" Gallery, Vilniaus St. 39
Vilniaus Jeruzalė Art Centre, Lobio St. 6a.
Arrangements for visiting should be made in advance by tel. 701291
"Znad Wilii", a gallery of Polish art, Išganytojo St. 2/4

## Cultural centres

British Council, Vilniaus St. 39/6
Centre of Cultural Activity of Eastern Lithuania, Jakšto St. 9–320
Centre of Lithuanian Folk Culture, Barboros Radvilaitės St. 8
Centre of Russian Culture, Išganytojo St. 2/4
Danish Culture Institute, Vilniaus St. 39/6
French Cultural Centre, Didžioji St. 1
Goethe Institut Vilnius – German Culture Institute, Tilto St. 3–6
Institute of Italian Culture, Universiteto St. 4
M.K. Čiurlionis House – cultural information centre, Savičiaus St. 11
Polish Institute, Švitrigailos St. 6/15
The American Centre of the US Embassy, Pranciškonų St. 3/6
UN Education, Science and Culture Organization – the Lithuanian
National UNESCO commission, Šv. Jono St. 11
Vilnius Centre of Ethnic Activity, Pamėnkalnio St. 34
Vilnius Teachers' House, Vilniaus St. 39/6

## Bookshops

"Akademinė knyga", Universiteto St. 4
"Draugystė", Gedimino Ave. 2
"Humanitas", Vokiečių St. 2
"Katalikų pasaulis", Dominikonų St. 6
"Littera", Šv. Jono St. 12 (at University)
"Pilies", Pilies St. 22
"Vilniaus centrinis", Gedimino Ave. 13
"Versmė", Didžioji St. 27

## Tourist information centres

Vilniaus St. 22, tel. 629660
Pilies St. 42, tel. 626470

# INDEX OF OBJECTS

# INDEX OF PERSONAL NAMES

The publisher is grateful to the following institutions
for their permission to use illustrations:

## Institute of the Lithuanian Literature and Folklore
(p. 40 ill. 3; p. 52 ill. 2, 3;  p. 60 ill. 4),

## Library of the Academy of Sciences
(ill. p. 15; p. 22 ill. 5; ill. p. 23; p. 36 ill. 4; p. 42 ill. 2, 4; ill. p. 45;  p. 50 ill. 3;
archive photos on p. 112, 154, 155 (2 ill.), 180, 190, 199),

## Library of Vilnius University
(p. 12 ill. 1, 3; p. 18 ill. 2; p. 20 ill. 5; p. 21 ill. 1, 2; p. 22 ill. 4; p. 29 ill. 1, 3, 4;
p. 31 ill. 1–3; p. 38 ill. 3; p. 44 ill. 4; ill. p. 53),

## Lithuanian Art Museum
(p. 8  ill. 2; p. 28 ill. 3–5; p. 34 ill. 1, 4; p. 36 ill. 3; p. 40 ill. 2; p. 48 ill. 3;
p. 50 ill. 2; archive photos on p. 81, 87),

## Lithuanian Audiovisual Archive
(p. 64 ill. 5; ill. p. 67),

## Lithuanian National Museum
(ill. p. 6, 7, 8; p. 10 ill. 1–6; ill. p. 11; p. 12 ill. 1, 3; p. 14  ill. 1, 2, 4;
p. 16 ill. 3–8; p. 20 ill. 1–3; p. 22 ill. 1–3; ill. p. 23; p. 24 ill. 1–4; ill. p. 25;
p. 26 ill. 4, 5; p. 28 ill. 1, 2; ill. p. 29; p. 28 ill. 2; p. 32 ill. 1, 5; ill. p. 33;
p. 34 ill. 3, 5; p. 36 ill. 1, 3, 5; p. 38 ill. 1, 2, 4; ill. p. 39; p. 40 ill. 1, 4–7;
p. 42 ill. 1, 3, 5, 6; ill. p. 43; p. 44 ill. 1–3, 4, 5; p. 46 ill. 1–6; ill. p. 47;
p. 48 ill. 5; ill. p. 49; p. 50 ill. 1; ill. p. 51; p. 52 ill. 1, 2; p. 54 ill. 1, 3–5;
p. 56 ill. 2–4; p. 58 ill. 1–3, 5, 6; p. 60 ill. 2; p. 62 ill. 1, 3, 4; ill. p. 63;
p. 64 ill. 1–3; ill. p. 65; archive photos on p. 167, 169, 173, 195),

## Museum of Theatre, Music and Cinema
(p. 48 ill. 1, 2, 4; p. 54 ill. 2; p. 60 ill. 1; ill. p. 61),

## Museum of Vilnius University
(p. 21 ill. 3; p. 26 ill. 3; archive photos on p. 161, 182),

## National M. K. Čiurlionis Art Museum
(p. 52 ill. 4),

## Vilnius Church of St. Peter and St. Paul
(p. 32 ill. 2),

## Vilnius Gaon Jewish Museum
(p. 32 ill. 4; p. 50 ill. 4; p. 62 ill. 2).

Tomas Venclova
# VILNIUS
City Guide

Publication sponsored
by the Ministry of Culture of Lithuania

Photographs
Arūnas Baltėnas, Raimondas Paknys,
Kęstutis Stoškus

Translated by
Aušra Simanavičiūtė

Edited by
Kazys Almenas

Consultants
Regimanta Stankevičienė, Evaldas Zilinskas,
Robertas Zilinskas

Art Director
Arūnas Baltėnas

Designer
Izaokas Zibucas

Layouts designed by
Briedis Publishers

Revised edition 2002
© R. Paknio leidykla, 2001, 2002

R. Paknys Publishing House
Išganytojo 4-10, 2001 Vilnius
tel. (+370 2) 629950
e-mail centras@paknioleidykla.lt
ISBN 9986-830-48-6